I0020992

VIRTUALIZATION POWER PACK
NOVICE TO NINJA

MASTERING VMWARE, VIRTUALBOX, PARALLELS, CITRIX

4 BOOKS IN 1

BOOK 1
VIRTUALIZATION ESSENTIALS: A BEGINNER'S GUIDE TO VMWARE

BOOK 2
MASTERING VIRTUALBOX: BUILDING AND MANAGING VIRTUAL ENVIRONMENTS

BOOK 3
ADVANCED VIRTUALIZATION WITH PARALLELS DESKTOP: OPTIMIZING FOR PRODUCTIVITY AND PERFORMANCE

BOOK 4
CITRIX HYPERVISOR MASTERY: EXPERT TECHNIQUES FOR VIRTUALIZATION PROFESSIONALS

ROB BOTWRIGHT

Copyright © 2023 by Rob Botwright
All rights reserved. No part of this book may be
reproduced or transmitted in any form or by any means,
electronic or mechanical, including photocopying,
recording, or by any information storage and retrieval
system, without permission in writing from the
publisher.

Published by Rob Botwright
Library of Congress Cataloging-in-Publication Data
ISBN 978-1-83938-579-7
Cover design by Rizzo

Disclaimer

The contents of this book are based on extensive research and the best available historical sources. However, the author and publisher make no claims, promises, or guarantees about the accuracy, completeness, or adequacy of the information contained herein. The information in this book is provided on an "as is" basis, and the author and publisher disclaim any and all liability for any errors, omissions, or inaccuracies in the information or for any actions taken in reliance on such information.

The opinions and views expressed in this book are those of the author and do not necessarily reflect the official policy or position of any organization or individual mentioned in this book. Any reference to specific people, places, or events is intended only to provide historical context and is not intended to defame or malign any group, individual, or entity.

The information in this book is intended for educational and entertainment purposes only. It is not intended to be a substitute for professional advice or judgment. Readers are encouraged to conduct their own research and to seek professional advice where appropriate.

Every effort has been made to obtain necessary permissions and acknowledgments for all images and other copyrighted material used in this book. Any errors or omissions in this regard are unintentional, and the author and publisher will correct them in future editions.

TABLE OF CONTENTS - BOOK 1 - VIRTUALIZATION ESSENTIALS: A BEGINNER'S GUIDE TO VMWARE

TABLE OF CONTENTS - BOOK 2 - MASTERING VIRTUALBOX: BUILDING AND MANAGING VIRTUAL ENVIRONMENTS

TABLE OF CONTENTS - BOOK 3 - ADVANCED VIRTUALIZATION WITH PARALLELS DESKTOP: OPTIMIZING FOR PRODUCTIVITY AND PERFORMANCE

TABLE OF CONTENTS - BOOK 4 - CITRIX HYPERVISOR MASTERY: EXPERT TECHNIQUES FOR VIRTUALIZATION PROFESSIONALS

Introduction

In the ever-evolving landscape of information technology, virtualization has emerged as a transformative force, reshaping the way we approach computing and data management. From the novice enthusiast to the seasoned IT professional, the power of virtualization offers a gateway to enhanced efficiency, flexibility, and resource optimization. With the "Virtualization Power Pack: Novice To Ninja," we embark on a journey through the realms of four leading virtualization technologies, equipping you with the knowledge and expertise to become a virtualization virtuoso.

This comprehensive bundle comprises four distinct books, each tailored to cater to a specific phase of your virtualization journey. Whether you're taking your first steps into the virtualization universe or aiming to master advanced techniques, this collection has you covered.

Book 1 - Virtualization Essentials: A Beginner's Guide to VMware: In this foundational volume, we lay the groundwork for your virtualization odyssey. Starting from square one, we introduce you to the core concepts of virtualization and provide an in-depth exploration of VMware, a leading virtualization platform. By the end of this book, you will have grasped the fundamentals, installed VMware, and created your initial virtual machine, setting the stage for your ascent from novice to ninja.

Book 2 - Mastering VirtualBox: Building and Managing Virtual Environments: As you progress, "Mastering VirtualBox" takes you deeper into the realm of virtualization. VirtualBox, a powerful and versatile platform, becomes your playground as you learn to install it, create virtual machines, and efficiently manage virtual environments. Armed with this knowledge, you'll be prepared to tackle a broad array of virtualization challenges.

Book 3 - Advanced Virtualization with Parallels Desktop: Optimizing for Productivity and Performance: With a solid foundation under your belt, we shift our focus to the macOS environment in "Advanced Virtualization with Parallels Desktop." Here, you'll discover how to seamlessly integrate Parallels Desktop with macOS, employing advanced storage management techniques and performance optimization strategies. By mastering Parallels, you'll harness the full potential of virtualization on Apple hardware.

Book 4 - Citrix Hypervisor Mastery: Expert Techniques for Virtualization Professionals: Finally, as you near the summit of virtualization proficiency, "Citrix Hypervisor Mastery" awaits. This book immerses you in the world of Citrix Hypervisor, an enterprise-grade virtualization platform. You'll explore advanced storage and networking, delve into high availability and load balancing, and unlock the secrets of snapshots, cloning, and backup strategies. With this expertise, you'll be prepared to excel in managing large-scale virtualization environments.

Each book in this power pack is designed to provide you with a comprehensive understanding of its respective virtualization technology. Whether your goal is to enhance your IT career, streamline your business operations, or simply satisfy your curiosity, the knowledge gained from this bundle will empower you to harness the incredible potential of virtualization.

So, whether you're taking your first step into the virtual world or are on a quest to become a virtualization ninja, fasten your seatbelt, and prepare for an exciting journey. The "Virtualization Power Pack: Novice To Ninja" is your ticket to unlocking the immense possibilities and benefits of virtualization technology. Let's embark on this transformative voyage together.

BOOK 1
VIRTUALIZATION ESSENTIALS
A BEGINNER'S GUIDE TO VMWARE

ROB BOTWRIGHT

Chapter 1: Introduction to Virtualization

Virtualization is a technology that has transformed the way we use and manage computing resources in recent years. It has become a fundamental concept in the world of IT, revolutionizing the way we deploy, manage, and utilize servers, storage, and even entire data centers. Virtualization enables the creation of multiple virtual instances or environments on a single physical server or host system, allowing for the efficient utilization of hardware resources and enhancing flexibility and scalability.

The concept of virtualization can be traced back to the early days of computing when researchers and engineers sought ways to maximize the use of expensive mainframe computers. However, it was in the late 20th century and early 21st century that virtualization truly came into its own, with the advent of powerful x86-based processors and hypervisor technologies.

At its core, virtualization involves creating a virtual layer or abstraction between the physical hardware and the software that runs on it. This virtual layer, often referred to as a hypervisor or virtual machine monitor (VMM), manages the allocation of physical resources to virtual machines (VMs). Each VM behaves like an independent computer with its own operating system and applications, but multiple VMs can coexist on the same physical server.

One of the key advantages of virtualization is resource consolidation. By running multiple VMs on a single physical server, organizations can make more efficient use of their hardware resources. This not only reduces the need for purchasing and maintaining numerous physical servers but also leads to cost savings in terms of power consumption, cooling, and physical space requirements.

Virtualization also brings flexibility to IT environments. VMs can be easily provisioned or de-provisioned, allowing for rapid scaling of resources as needed. This agility is particularly valuable in cloud computing and data center environments, where workloads can fluctuate significantly.

Furthermore, virtualization enhances disaster recovery and business continuity planning. VMs can be replicated to remote locations, providing a level of redundancy that can help ensure data and application availability even in the face of hardware failures or disasters. This has become a critical aspect of modern IT infrastructure design.

There are several types of virtualization, each serving specific purposes. Server virtualization, for example, involves running multiple VMs on a single physical server. This is perhaps the most common form of virtualization and is widely used in data centers to maximize server utilization.

Desktop virtualization, on the other hand, extends the benefits of virtualization to end-user computing. It allows for the centralization of desktop environments, making it easier to manage and secure user workspaces.

Storage virtualization abstracts and pools physical storage resources, providing a more flexible and efficient way to manage storage infrastructure.

Network virtualization separates network resources from the underlying physical hardware, enabling the creation of virtual networks that can be customized and segmented to meet specific needs.

In addition to these common forms of virtualization, there are also application virtualization, containerization, and even virtualization at the network function level (NFV) in telecommunications.

While virtualization offers numerous advantages, it also presents challenges. Managing a virtualized environment can be complex, as administrators must oversee not only the physical hardware but also the many VMs running on it.

Security is another concern, as vulnerabilities in one VM could potentially impact others on the same host.

Performance optimization and resource allocation are ongoing tasks, as administrators must ensure that VMs receive the necessary resources to operate efficiently.

Over the years, various virtualization technologies and management tools have emerged to address these challenges.

Leading virtualization vendors such as VMware, Microsoft, and Citrix have developed robust hypervisor solutions and management platforms that simplify the deployment and administration of virtualized environments.

In recent years, containerization technologies like Docker have gained popularity for application deployment and management, complementing traditional virtualization approaches.

These technologies provide lightweight, portable, and isolated containers that can run applications and their dependencies in a consistent manner across different environments.

As virtualization continues to evolve, it plays a critical role in the development of cloud computing and hybrid cloud solutions.

Cloud providers leverage virtualization to deliver scalable and on-demand services to customers, while organizations adopt hybrid cloud models that combine on-premises infrastructure with public and private cloud resources.

In summary, virtualization has transformed the IT landscape, offering a flexible and efficient way to maximize the utilization of hardware resources and improve the agility of IT environments.

It has become a fundamental technology for modern data centers, cloud computing, and various other IT deployments.

Understanding the concepts and benefits of virtualization is essential for IT professionals and organizations looking to harness the power of this transformative technology in their operations. Virtualization, as a technology, has brought about a profound transformation in the world of information technology and computing. It has redefined the way we utilize and manage our computing resources, offering numerous benefits and applications that have become integral to the modern IT landscape. At its core, virtualization involves the abstraction of physical hardware, allowing multiple virtual instances or environments to run on a single physical server or host system.

One of the foremost benefits of virtualization is resource optimization. Through the efficient allocation of hardware resources to virtual machines (VMs), organizations can significantly improve their hardware utilization, leading to cost savings in terms of reduced power consumption, cooling, and physical space requirements. This consolidation of resources is particularly valuable in data center environments, where the demand for computing power continues to grow.

Moreover, virtualization enhances flexibility and agility in IT operations. By creating virtual machines, organizations can quickly provision or de-provision computing resources as needed, responding dynamically to changing workload demands. This ability to scale resources rapidly is invaluable in cloud computing environments, where elasticity is a fundamental requirement.

Another compelling advantage of virtualization is its contribution to disaster recovery and business continuity strategies. Virtual machines can be replicated to remote locations, providing redundancy and ensuring that critical applications and data remain accessible, even in the event of hardware failures or natural disasters. This redundancy enhances the overall resilience of IT infrastructure.

Furthermore, virtualization simplifies the management of computing environments. With the ability to encapsulate entire operating systems and applications within VMs, administrators can more easily deploy, manage, and maintain systems. This centralization of management tasks reduces complexity and streamlines IT operations.

In the realm of desktop computing, virtualization extends its benefits to end-users. Desktop virtualization solutions, such as Virtual Desktop Infrastructure (VDI), enable organizations to centralize desktop environments, making them easier to manage, secure, and deliver to users. This approach enhances security, simplifies updates, and allows for the efficient provisioning of desktops.

Storage virtualization is another facet of virtualization that delivers significant advantages. It abstracts and pools physical storage resources, enabling organizations to manage storage infrastructure more efficiently. With features like thin provisioning and dynamic storage allocation, storage virtualization helps organizations optimize their storage utilization and reduce costs. Additionally, network virtualization separates network resources from the underlying physical hardware, providing the ability to create virtual networks that can be customized to meet specific needs. This abstraction enhances network flexibility, security, and scalability. In the context of application delivery, virtualization offers the concept of application virtualization. This approach encapsulates applications and their dependencies into isolated containers, ensuring that they can run consistently across different environments. This enhances compatibility, simplifies application deployment, and reduces conflicts.

Containerization technologies, such as Docker and Kubernetes, have gained popularity for their ability to deliver lightweight, portable, and isolated containers for deploying and managing applications. Containers offer advantages in terms of efficiency, scalability, and reproducibility.

In the telecommunications industry, Network Function Virtualization (NFV) utilizes virtualization to replace traditional hardware-based network functions with software-based counterparts. This approach enhances network agility and scalability, leading to cost savings and improved service delivery.

Cloud computing, a pivotal development in the IT landscape, heavily relies on virtualization. Cloud providers leverage virtualization to create a pool of shared computing resources that can be dynamically allocated to customers as needed. This model offers tremendous scalability, elasticity, and cost-efficiency.

Hybrid cloud solutions, which combine on-premises infrastructure with public and private cloud resources, have also become prevalent. Virtualization plays a crucial role in seamlessly integrating and managing resources across hybrid environments.

In summary, virtualization has become an indispensable technology, revolutionizing the way we utilize computing resources and manage IT environments. Its benefits extend across various domains, from resource optimization and flexibility to enhanced disaster recovery, simplified management, and improved security.

Virtualization has paved the way for innovations like desktop virtualization, storage virtualization, network virtualization, and containerization, each offering specific advantages in different contexts. As organizations continue to embrace cloud computing and hybrid cloud models, virtualization remains at the core, enabling the dynamic allocation of resources and driving the evolution of modern IT infrastructure.

Understanding the broad spectrum of virtualization benefits and applications is crucial for IT professionals and organizations seeking to harness the full potential of this transformative technology in their operations.

Chapter 2: Understanding VMware Basics

VMware, a pioneer in the field of virtualization, is known for its powerful suite of products and technologies that have redefined the way we deploy and manage IT infrastructure. To grasp the essence of VMware, it's essential to explore its core concepts, which form the foundation of its virtualization solutions. At the heart of VMware's virtualization offerings is the concept of the hypervisor, a software layer that abstracts and virtualizes the physical hardware, enabling the creation of multiple virtual machines (VMs) on a single physical server.

The hypervisor acts as a mediator, efficiently allocating physical resources such as CPU, memory, and storage to the VMs running on the host system. VMware offers two main types of hypervisors: Type 1, also known as a bare-metal hypervisor, runs directly on the physical hardware without the need for a host operating system, while Type 2, or hosted hypervisors, run on top of an existing operating system.

VMware's flagship product, VMware vSphere, is built upon this fundamental hypervisor technology. It provides a comprehensive platform for virtualization, encompassing compute, storage, and networking virtualization. vSphere enables organizations to create, manage, and optimize virtualized data centers, making it a cornerstone of modern IT infrastructure.

Within the vSphere ecosystem, one encounters the concept of the vCenter Server, a centralized management platform that plays a pivotal role in administering VMware environments. vCenter Server provides a unified interface for managing multiple hosts and VMs, simplifying tasks such as provisioning, monitoring, and resource allocation.

VMware also offers a range of virtualization solutions tailored to specific use cases. VMware Workstation, for example, is a desktop virtualization product that allows developers and IT professionals to run multiple operating systems on a single physical machine, facilitating testing, development, and troubleshooting tasks.

For server virtualization, VMware vSphere Hypervisor (formerly known as VMware ESXi) is a powerful, free-to-use hypervisor that serves as the foundation for building virtualized data centers. It offers features such as high availability, live migration, and resource pooling.

VMware vSAN (Virtual Storage Area Network) extends the virtualization paradigm to storage, abstracting and pooling storage devices across multiple hosts to create a highly scalable and efficient storage infrastructure. It simplifies storage management and reduces the need for costly and complex storage area networks (SANs).

Networking virtualization is another crucial aspect of VMware's offerings. VMware NSX is a software-defined networking (SDN) solution that abstracts and virtualizes network resources, enabling the creation of virtual networks that are agile, secure, and highly scalable. NSX empowers organizations to automate network provisioning, micro-segmentation, and network security policies.

In addition to these core concepts, VMware embraces the concept of cloud computing. VMware Cloud enables organizations to extend their virtualized environments to public, private, or hybrid clouds seamlessly. This flexibility enables businesses to leverage cloud resources while maintaining consistency and control over their workloads.

VMware's commitment to innovation is exemplified by its ongoing development of technologies such as VMware Tanzu, which focuses on containerization and Kubernetes orchestration, and VMware Cloud Foundation, an integrated platform for hybrid cloud infrastructure.

As virtualization technology continues to evolve, VMware remains at the forefront, consistently pushing the boundaries of what is possible in IT infrastructure management and virtualization. Understanding VMware's core concepts is essential for IT professionals and organizations seeking to harness the full potential of virtualization to enhance agility, reduce costs, and transform their IT operations.

In summary, VMware's core concepts, including the hypervisor, vSphere, vCenter Server, and specialized solutions like vSAN and NSX, form the bedrock of its virtualization offerings. These concepts enable organizations to build, manage, and optimize their IT environments efficiently, driving innovation and flexibility in today's ever-evolving digital landscape.

Key components of VMware technology are at the heart of the company's virtualization solutions, forming the building blocks that enable the creation and management of virtualized environments.

At the core of VMware's offerings is the hypervisor, a critical piece of software that abstracts physical hardware resources, allowing multiple virtual machines (VMs) to run on a single physical server.

VMware offers two primary types of hypervisors: Type 1, also known as a bare-metal hypervisor, runs directly on the physical hardware, while Type 2, or hosted hypervisors, run on top of an existing operating system.

The hypervisor serves as a fundamental layer that manages resource allocation, enabling efficient sharing of CPU, memory, storage, and networking capabilities among VMs.

VMware's flagship product, VMware vSphere, extends the capabilities of the hypervisor to create a comprehensive platform for data center virtualization.

Within the vSphere ecosystem, one of the key components is the vCenter Server, a centralized management platform that plays a pivotal role in administering VMware environments.

vCenter Server provides a unified interface for managing multiple hosts and VMs, simplifying tasks such as provisioning, monitoring, and resource allocation.

Another critical component of VMware technology is the vSphere Client, a user-friendly web-based interface that allows administrators to interact with their virtualized environments.

The vSphere Client offers a rich set of tools and features for managing VMs, configuring networking, and monitoring performance.

VMware Workstation is a desktop virtualization product that caters to developers and IT professionals, providing them with the ability to run multiple operating systems on a single physical machine.

This key component facilitates tasks such as software development, testing, and troubleshooting in a sandboxed environment.

For server virtualization, VMware offers vSphere Hypervisor, formerly known as VMware ESXi, a powerful and free-to-use hypervisor that serves as the foundation for building virtualized data centers.

vSphere Hypervisor offers features such as high availability, live migration, and resource pooling, making it an essential component for organizations looking to optimize their server infrastructure.

Storage virtualization is another crucial aspect of VMware technology, with VMware vSAN leading the way.

vSAN, which stands for Virtual Storage Area Network, abstracts and pools storage devices across multiple hosts, creating a scalable and efficient storage infrastructure.

This component simplifies storage management, reduces the reliance on complex storage area networks (SANs), and enhances the overall performance of virtualized environments.

Networking virtualization is also integral to VMware's offerings, and VMware NSX is the key component in this domain.

NSX, or Network Virtualization and Security, abstracts and virtualizes network resources, allowing organizations to create agile, secure, and scalable virtual networks.

This component enables automation of network provisioning, micro-segmentation, and the enforcement of network security policies.

VMware's commitment to innovation is evident through its development of technologies like VMware Tanzu, which focuses on containerization and Kubernetes orchestration.

Tanzu empowers organizations to deploy, manage, and scale containerized applications seamlessly within their VMware environments.

In addition to Tanzu, VMware Cloud Foundation is another notable key component that provides an integrated platform for hybrid cloud infrastructure.

This component facilitates the deployment and management of cloud-based resources while maintaining consistency and control over workloads.

As virtualization technology continues to evolve, VMware remains a leader in the field, consistently pushing the boundaries of what is achievable in IT infrastructure management and virtualization.

Understanding the key components of VMware technology is essential for IT professionals and organizations seeking to harness the full potential of virtualization to enhance agility, reduce costs, and transform their IT operations.

In summary, VMware's key components, including the hypervisor, vSphere, vCenter Server, vSphere Client, VMware Workstation, vSphere Hypervisor, vSAN, NSX, Tanzu, and VMware Cloud Foundation, form the bedrock of its virtualization and cloud solutions.

These components work in harmony to enable organizations to build, manage, and optimize their IT environments efficiently, driving innovation and flexibility in today's ever-evolving digital landscape.

Chapter 3: Installing VMware

Preparing your system for VMware installation is a crucial step to ensure a smooth and successful deployment of virtualization technology. Before diving into the installation process, it's essential to assess your hardware and software prerequisites.

Start by verifying that your hardware meets the requirements specified by VMware for the version you intend to install. Check the processor, memory, and storage capacity to ensure they meet or exceed the minimum recommended specifications.

Keep in mind that different VMware products may have specific hardware requirements, so consult the official documentation for the product you plan to install.

In addition to hardware requirements, software compatibility is a critical consideration. Ensure that your operating system, network configuration, and other software components are compatible with the VMware product you intend to install.

Review the VMware Compatibility Guide to confirm that your hardware and software components are officially supported. This step can help prevent compatibility issues that may arise during or after the installation process.

Next, consider the storage requirements for your VMware installation. Plan for sufficient storage capacity to accommodate the virtual machines you intend to create and manage.

Keep in mind that storage performance can significantly impact the overall performance of your virtualized environment, so choose storage solutions that align with your performance goals.

It's advisable to allocate separate storage for virtual machine files, configuration files, and logs to maintain organization and optimize performance.

Network configuration is another crucial aspect of preparing your system for VMware installation. Ensure that your network infrastructure is properly configured to support the desired networking features and capabilities of the VMware product.

Review your network switches, routers, and firewalls to identify any potential bottlenecks or areas that may require optimization for virtualization.

Consider the IP address allocation for your virtual machines, as well as any networking features such as VLANs, load balancing, and network security policies.

When planning your network configuration, keep scalability and redundancy in mind to ensure the long-term stability of your virtualized environment.

Before proceeding with the installation, it's essential to perform a thorough backup of your existing system.

Creating a backup ensures that you have a restore point in case anything goes wrong during the installation or configuration process.

Backup your operating system, important data, and any critical configurations to an external storage device or a remote location.

Ensure that you have the necessary installation media or software packages readily available.

Download the VMware product installation files from the official VMware website or obtain them from authorized sources.

Having the installation files on hand streamlines the installation process and prevents delays due to downloading large files during the installation.

Also, prepare any required license keys or activation codes, as they may be necessary during the installation and configuration.

Consider the network connectivity of your installation environment.

Ensure that the system where you plan to install VMware has access to the internet or required network resources to fetch updates, patches, and additional software components during the installation.

If your environment has limited or restricted internet access, plan for alternative methods of obtaining necessary files and updates.

Finally, document your installation plan and configuration decisions.

Having clear and well-documented plans helps streamline the installation process and serves as a reference point in case of issues or future upgrades.

Include details such as hardware specifications, software versions, network configurations, and any custom settings you plan to apply during the installation.

By following these steps and thoroughly preparing your system for VMware installation, you set the foundation for a successful virtualization deployment.

Taking the time to assess your hardware and software requirements, configure your network, and ensure proper backup and documentation will contribute to a smooth and efficient installation process.

The step-by-step VMware installation process is a critical part of deploying virtualization technology in your environment. It involves several stages, each carefully executed to ensure a successful installation.

First, insert the installation media or mount the ISO file containing the VMware software on the target server or workstation.

If you are using a physical installation media, such as a DVD, ensure it is properly inserted into the optical drive. Alternatively, if you are using an ISO file, mount it as a virtual optical drive on the host system.

Next, power on or boot the target server or workstation, and access the system's BIOS or UEFI settings.

In the BIOS or UEFI settings, configure the system to boot from the installation media or virtual optical drive where the VMware software is located.

Save the changes and exit the BIOS or UEFI settings, allowing the system to boot from the installation media.

As the system boots from the installation media, you will be presented with the VMware installation wizard.

The installation wizard will guide you through the necessary steps to install the VMware software on your system.

Select the appropriate language and keyboard layout for the installation process.

This ensures that the installation wizard's prompts and messages are displayed in the preferred language and that keyboard input is correctly interpreted.

Choose the option to install VMware.

Depending on the VMware product you are installing, the exact wording may vary, but it will generally be labeled as an option for installation.

The installation wizard will then present you with the option to either install a fresh copy or upgrade an existing installation of VMware.

Select the appropriate option based on your requirements. If you are performing a fresh installation, the wizard will guide you through partitioning and formatting the system's storage devices.

Choose the destination drive or partition where you want to install VMware.

In most cases, VMware will recommend a default installation location, but you can customize it if necessary.

The installation wizard will prompt you to confirm your selection, as installing VMware will overwrite any existing data on the selected drive or partition.

Confirm your choice to proceed with the installation.

The installation process will begin, and you will see a progress bar indicating the installation status.

This step may take some time, depending on the speed of your system and the size of the VMware installation files.

During the installation, the wizard may prompt you to provide certain configuration details, such as the root password or administrator credentials.

Ensure that you choose strong and secure passwords to protect your VMware installation.

Once the installation is complete, the wizard will prompt you to remove the installation media or unmount the ISO file if necessary.

Follow the instructions to complete this step.

After removing the installation media, the system will reboot automatically.

Allow the system to boot from the newly installed VMware software.

Upon booting, VMware may perform additional configuration tasks, such as initializing system services and drivers.

This phase of the installation process is automatic and may take a few moments to complete.

Once the system has fully booted into VMware, you will be presented with the login screen.

Enter the root password or the administrator credentials that you provided during the installation.

After successfully logging in, you will have access to the VMware environment, where you can start configuring virtual machines, networking, and storage according to your needs.

At this point, the basic installation of VMware is complete, and you can begin using the virtualization platform to create and manage virtual machines.

It's important to note that the exact steps and prompts may vary slightly depending on the specific VMware product you are installing and the version you are using.

Always refer to the official VMware documentation for the product-specific installation instructions and any additional configuration steps that may be required.

In summary, the step-by-step VMware installation process involves booting from the installation media, selecting installation options, configuring storage, providing necessary credentials, and completing the installation.

Once the installation is successful, you can log in to the VMware environment and begin utilizing its virtualization capabilities to create and manage virtual machines and other resources.

Chapter 4: Creating Your First Virtual Machine

Virtual machine creation fundamentals are at the core of virtualization technology, enabling the deployment of multiple virtual environments on a single physical server. Understanding the key principles and best practices for creating virtual machines is essential for efficiently harnessing the power of virtualization.

At the heart of virtual machine creation is the concept of abstraction, where the physical hardware of a server is separated from the software that runs on it. This abstraction is facilitated by a hypervisor, a software layer that acts as a mediator between the physical hardware and the virtual machines.

Before creating a virtual machine, it's essential to plan and define its characteristics, such as the desired operating system, memory allocation, CPU resources, and storage requirements. This initial planning phase sets the foundation for a well-structured virtual machine.

Selecting the appropriate operating system for your virtual machine is a critical decision, as it determines the software environment in which your applications will run. Ensure that the chosen operating system is compatible with the hypervisor and the software you intend to deploy.

Memory allocation is another crucial consideration when creating a virtual machine. Allocate an appropriate amount of memory to meet the requirements of the applications and services running within the VM. Be mindful of the available physical memory on the host server to avoid resource contention.

CPU resources play a significant role in the performance of a virtual machine. Assign the appropriate number of virtual CPUs (vCPUs) based on the workload demands. Keep in mind that over-allocating vCPUs can lead to resource contention and reduced performance.

Storage requirements should be carefully evaluated when creating virtual machines. Determine the amount of storage space needed for the operating system, applications, and data. Utilize storage best practices, such as thin provisioning and storage optimization, to maximize efficiency.

Consider the placement of virtual machine files, including the virtual hard disk (VHD) or virtual machine disk (VMDK) files. Storing virtual machine files on high-performance storage devices can improve overall performance.

When creating a virtual machine, it's important to specify the network configuration. Determine whether the VM will have its own network interface or share the host's network connection. Networking features like VLANs and virtual switches can be configured to isolate and secure VM traffic.

Choose an appropriate name and location for your virtual machine to ensure organization and easy identification. Consistent naming conventions can help manage virtual machines effectively in large environments.

Virtual machine templates and cloning provide efficient ways to create multiple virtual machines with similar configurations. Templates capture a predefined VM configuration, while cloning creates copies of an existing VM. These techniques save time and ensure consistency.

During the virtual machine creation process, you can define hardware resources, such as memory, CPU, and storage, either manually or by selecting predefined profiles. Profiles offer predefined resource allocations based on common use cases.

It's crucial to set security measures when creating virtual machines. Implement security policies, firewalls, and access controls within the VM to protect against unauthorized access and vulnerabilities.

Regularly update and patch the operating system and software within your virtual machines to address security vulnerabilities and ensure optimal performance.

Virtual machine snapshots provide a point-in-time backup of a VM's state. Use snapshots before making significant changes or updates to the VM, allowing you to roll back to a previous state if needed.

Monitoring and performance tuning are ongoing processes in virtual machine management. Monitor resource utilization, troubleshoot performance issues, and adjust resource allocations as necessary to optimize VM performance.

Virtual machine backup and disaster recovery plans should be in place to protect your VMs and data. Regularly back up virtual machines and test disaster recovery procedures to ensure business continuity.

Consider automation and orchestration tools to streamline the virtual machine creation process, especially in large-scale environments. Automation can help deploy and manage VMs efficiently.

In summary, virtual machine creation fundamentals encompass the planning, configuration, and management of virtual machines within a virtualization environment. Understanding these fundamentals is essential for deploying and maintaining virtualized infrastructure effectively. By following best practices and principles, organizations can harness the full potential of virtualization technology to improve efficiency, scalability, and resource utilization.

Creating your initial virtual machine is an exciting step in harnessing the power of virtualization technology for your specific needs. Whether you are setting up a virtual server, a development environment, or a testing environment, the process of creating your first virtual machine follows a set of essential steps.

Start by launching your chosen virtualization platform, such as VMware vSphere, VirtualBox, or Hyper-V. This software serves as the foundation for managing and creating virtual machines.

Once your virtualization platform is up and running, access the virtual machine management interface or console. This interface is where you will initiate the creation process.

Select the option to create a new virtual machine. This action typically opens a wizard or dialog box that guides you through the steps necessary to configure and customize your virtual machine.

The first step in creating your virtual machine is selecting the type or category of operating system you plan to install. This choice helps the virtualization platform apply appropriate settings and optimizations for your chosen OS.

Choose the version of the operating system you intend to install. Be precise, as different versions may require distinct configurations and settings.

Specify the name and location for your virtual machine. This information helps you identify and organize your virtual machines, especially when managing multiple instances.

Allocate memory or RAM to your virtual machine. Consider the memory requirements of your chosen operating system and any applications you plan to run within the VM.

Configure the number of virtual processors or CPU cores assigned to the virtual machine. This decision should align with the workload and performance requirements of your VM.

Create a virtual hard disk or select an existing one if you have a preconfigured disk image. The virtual hard disk serves as the storage space for your virtual machine's operating system and data.

Specify the size of the virtual hard disk, considering the storage needs of your OS and applications. Be mindful of your available physical storage capacity.

Select the type of virtual hard disk, such as fixed-size or dynamically allocated. Fixed-size disks consume all allocated space immediately, while dynamically allocated disks grow as needed.

Define the network configuration for your virtual machine. Choose between bridged, NAT, or host-only networking, depending on your connectivity requirements.

Review your virtual machine's settings and configuration choices to ensure they align with your intended use case. Make any necessary adjustments before proceeding.

Once you have configured the initial settings, initiate the creation process. Your virtualization platform will create the virtual machine based on your specifications.

Install the operating system on your virtual machine using installation media, such as an ISO image or a bootable CD/DVD. Follow the installation prompts and provide the required information.

During the OS installation, set up user accounts, passwords, and other configuration details as needed. These settings will be specific to the operating system you are installing.

After the OS installation is complete, install any necessary software, applications, or tools within your virtual machine. Customize the virtual machine to meet your specific requirements.

Consider taking a snapshot of your virtual machine's current state once you have completed the initial configuration and software installation. Snapshots serve as restore points, allowing you to return to a specific state if needed.

Test your virtual machine thoroughly to ensure that it functions as expected. Verify that all applications and services operate correctly within the virtual environment.

Implement security measures, such as firewalls and antivirus software, to protect your virtual machine and its contents from potential threats.

Regularly update and patch your virtual machine's operating system and installed software to address security vulnerabilities and maintain optimal performance.

Implement backup and disaster recovery strategies for your virtual machine to protect against data loss and system failures.

Document your virtual machine's configuration, including settings, software, and customizations, to serve as a reference and guide for future management and troubleshooting.

In summary, creating your initial virtual machine involves a series of steps that encompass choosing the operating system, configuring hardware resources, installing software, and implementing security measures. By following these steps and best practices, you can create a functional and customized virtual machine tailored to your specific needs. Virtual machines are versatile tools that enable you to run multiple operating systems and applications on a single physical host, making them invaluable for various use cases, from software development and testing to server consolidation and virtualization labs.

Chapter 5: Configuring Virtual Networks

Virtual networking is a fundamental component of modern computing environments, enabling the creation of virtual networks that operate independently of physical hardware. These virtual networks provide connectivity and communication between virtual machines (VMs) and external resources. Virtual networking offers several key concepts and capabilities that are essential to understand.

At the core of virtual networking is the concept of network virtualization, which abstracts and decouples network resources from physical hardware. This abstraction allows for the creation of multiple isolated virtual networks on the same physical infrastructure.

Each virtual network operates as an independent entity, with its own set of IP addresses, subnets, and network policies. This isolation ensures that VMs within one virtual network do not interfere with or have access to VMs in other virtual networks.

Virtual switches play a crucial role in virtual networking. These software-based switches route network traffic between VMs, allowing them to communicate with each other and with external networks. Virtual switches operate within the hypervisor and are responsible for forwarding data packets to the appropriate destinations.

One of the key advantages of virtual networking is network segmentation, which allows organizations to divide their virtual infrastructure into distinct segments or virtual LANs (VLANs). VLANs enable the logical separation of network traffic for different purposes, such as separating production and development environments or isolating sensitive data.

Another important concept in virtual networking is the idea of network overlays. Network overlays create virtual networks on top of physical networks, enabling the creation of logical networks that are independent of the underlying physical infrastructure. This abstraction simplifies network management and enhances flexibility.

Network Address Translation (NAT) is a technique used in virtual networking to map private IP addresses within a virtual network to a single public IP address for outbound traffic. NAT enables multiple VMs to share a single public IP address, conserving IPv4 address space.

Virtual networking also supports the creation of virtual routers and gateways, which serve as the entry and exit points for traffic between virtual networks and external networks. These virtual devices route traffic based on network policies and provide connectivity to the outside world.

Load balancing is a critical capability in virtual networking, allowing traffic to be distributed evenly across multiple VMs or servers. Load balancers enhance availability, scalability, and performance of applications by directing incoming requests to the most suitable server.

Virtual Private Networks (VPNs) are used in virtual networking to establish secure communication between remote users or sites and the virtual infrastructure. VPNs encrypt traffic and ensure data privacy and security.

Software-defined networking (SDN) is a technology that enhances virtual networking by centralizing network control and management. SDN controllers enable dynamic network provisioning and configuration, making it easier to adapt to changing workloads and traffic patterns.

Security is a paramount concern in virtual networking. Firewalls, intrusion detection systems (IDS), and intrusion prevention systems (IPS) are essential components for safeguarding virtual networks against threats and unauthorized access.

To manage virtual networking effectively, administrators use network management tools and consoles provided by virtualization platforms. These tools allow for the configuration, monitoring, and troubleshooting of virtual networks, ensuring their reliability and performance.

Network policies and access controls define the rules and permissions governing network traffic within virtual networks. These policies determine which VMs can communicate with each other and with external networks and help enforce security measures.

Virtual networking technologies have revolutionized the way organizations design and manage their IT infrastructures. By decoupling network resources from physical hardware, virtual networking provides flexibility, scalability, and agility to adapt to evolving business needs.

In summary, virtual networking is a vital aspect of modern computing environments, offering the ability to create isolated virtual networks that operate independently of physical hardware. Understanding the key concepts and capabilities of virtual networking is essential for effectively managing and securing virtualized infrastructure. These concepts, such as network virtualization, virtual switches, VLANs, network overlays, NAT, load balancing, virtual routers, and SDN, provide the foundation for building efficient and secure virtual networks that meet the demands of today's dynamic IT landscape.

Setting up virtual networks is a crucial step in harnessing the power of virtualization technology, allowing you to create isolated and interconnected network environments within your virtual infrastructure. The process involves several key considerations and steps to ensure that your virtual networks are well-configured and meet your specific requirements.

Begin by accessing the virtualization platform or hypervisor where you intend to create virtual networks. This platform serves as the foundation for managing virtual machines (VMs) and their associated networks.

In the virtualization platform's management interface, navigate to the networking section or virtual network manager, where you can configure and manage virtual networks. Here, you will find options for creating, configuring, and connecting virtual networks.

Determine the type of virtual network you need to set up based on your specific use case. Virtual networks can be categorized into various types, including internal networks, host-only networks, bridged networks, and more. The choice of network type depends on your connectivity and isolation requirements.

Internal networks are entirely isolated from external networks and other virtual networks, making them suitable for creating isolated test environments or virtual labs. Host-only networks allow communication between VMs on the same host but not with external networks. Bridged networks connect VMs to the external physical network, allowing them to communicate with other devices on the same network.

Create the virtual network by specifying its name and configuring its properties. You can assign IP address ranges, subnets, and other network settings to define the network's characteristics.

Consider using network segmentation to logically divide your virtual infrastructure into separate network segments or virtual LANs (VLANs). VLANs enable the isolation of traffic for different purposes, such as separating development and production environments or segregating sensitive data.

Virtual switches play a vital role in virtual network configuration, as they act as the network bridges that connect VMs within a virtual network and route traffic between them. Configure virtual switches to define the connectivity between VMs and the external network.

In many virtualization platforms, you can create multiple virtual switches, each serving a specific purpose or connecting to different physical network interfaces. This flexibility allows you to design complex network topologies tailored to your requirements.

Consider setting up network overlays, which create virtual networks on top of physical networks, providing an additional layer of abstraction. Overlays allow for the creation of logical networks that are independent of the underlying physical infrastructure, simplifying network management.

Implement Network Address Translation (NAT) if you need to allow VMs in an isolated network to access external resources, such as the internet. NAT maps private IP addresses within the virtual network to a single public IP address for outbound traffic, conserving IPv4 address space.

Ensure that your virtual networks have adequate security measures in place. Implement firewalls, intrusion detection systems (IDS), and intrusion prevention systems (IPS) to protect against unauthorized access and network threats.

Create and configure virtual routers and gateways to enable communication between virtual networks and external networks. These virtual devices route traffic based on network policies and provide connectivity to the outside world.

Load balancing is an essential capability for distributing network traffic evenly across multiple VMs or servers. Load balancers enhance availability, scalability, and performance by directing incoming requests to the most suitable server.

Consider implementing Virtual Private Networks (VPNs) to establish secure communication between remote users or sites and your virtual infrastructure. VPNs encrypt traffic and ensure data privacy and security.

Regularly monitor and maintain your virtual networks to ensure optimal performance and security. Use network management tools and consoles provided by your virtualization platform to configure, monitor, and troubleshoot virtual networks effectively.

Document your virtual network configurations, including settings, IP address ranges, VLAN assignments, and security policies. Having clear and well-documented network documentation helps streamline network management and troubleshooting.

In summary, setting up virtual networks is a critical aspect of virtualization technology, allowing you to create isolated and interconnected network environments tailored to your specific needs. Understanding the key considerations and steps involved in configuring virtual networks is essential for efficiently managing and securing your virtualized infrastructure. Virtual networks provide flexibility, scalability, and agility to adapt to changing business requirements and enable the efficient operation of virtual machines and applications.

Chapter 6: Managing Virtual Storage

Working with virtual storage is a fundamental aspect of managing virtualized environments, as it enables the efficient allocation and management of storage resources for virtual machines (VMs). Virtual storage solutions offer flexibility, scalability, and cost-effectiveness, making them a crucial component in modern IT infrastructure.

Virtualization abstracts physical storage devices and presents them as virtual storage to VMs. This abstraction allows multiple VMs to share the same physical storage resources while maintaining isolation and security.

One of the primary benefits of virtual storage is the ability to allocate storage on-demand, allowing VMs to access the storage capacity they need when they need it. This dynamic allocation optimizes resource utilization and simplifies storage management.

Virtual storage also supports features like thin provisioning, which allocates storage space to VMs only as they consume it, eliminating the need to pre-allocate large amounts of storage upfront. Thin provisioning helps conserve storage resources and reduces wasted capacity.

Snapshots are a valuable feature of virtual storage, enabling the creation of point-in-time copies of VMs or storage volumes. Snapshots serve as backups and provide a convenient way to revert to a previous state if data corruption or errors occur.

When working with virtual storage, administrators can leverage storage management tools and interfaces provided by virtualization platforms. These tools allow for the creation, allocation, resizing, and monitoring of virtual storage resources.

Consider implementing storage pools or storage clusters to aggregate and manage storage resources efficiently. Storage pools allow for the pooling of storage devices, simplifying storage management and enhancing scalability.

Virtual storage supports the use of different storage types, such as network-attached storage (NAS) and storage area networks (SANs). NAS provides file-level storage access, making it suitable for sharing files and data among VMs. SAN, on the other hand, offers block-level storage access, which is ideal for high-performance workloads and applications.

Storage tiers are used to categorize and manage storage resources based on performance and cost considerations. High-performance storage tiers, such as solid-state drives (SSDs), are suitable for critical applications that require low latency and high I/O performance. Lower-cost storage tiers, like traditional hard disk drives (HDDs), are suitable for less demanding workloads.

Data deduplication and compression are storage optimization techniques that reduce storage space requirements by eliminating redundant data and compressing data to occupy less space. These techniques help maximize storage efficiency and reduce costs.

Storage snapshots, a feature provided by many virtual storage solutions, allow for the creation of read-only copies of storage volumes or VMs at a specific point in time. Snapshots serve as backups and can be used for data recovery or testing without affecting the production environment.

Backup and disaster recovery strategies are essential when working with virtual storage. Regularly back up virtual storage volumes and VMs to protect against data loss and system failures. Test disaster recovery procedures to ensure business continuity.

Storage replication is another valuable capability in virtual storage, allowing data to be duplicated and synchronized across multiple storage devices or locations. Replication enhances data availability and provides redundancy in case of hardware failures.

Consider implementing storage tiering, which involves categorizing data based on its access patterns and importance. Frequently accessed and critical data can be stored on high-performance storage tiers, while less frequently accessed data can reside on lower-cost storage tiers.

Storage policies and access controls define how storage resources are allocated and accessed by VMs. Implement policies to ensure that VMs receive the appropriate storage resources and that data remains secure and compliant with regulatory requirements.

Storage snapshots provide a point-in-time backup of storage volumes, allowing for data recovery and rollback to a previous state in case of data corruption or errors.

In summary, working with virtual storage is a critical aspect of managing virtualized environments, offering flexibility, efficiency, and scalability in storage resource allocation. Virtual storage solutions enable organizations to optimize storage utilization, implement data protection strategies, and support diverse storage types and optimization techniques. By understanding the principles and features of virtual storage, administrators can effectively manage and optimize storage resources to meet the demands of modern IT environments.

Managing storage in VMware is a vital aspect of maintaining an efficient and reliable virtualized environment. Properly configuring, monitoring, and optimizing storage resources ensures that virtual machines (VMs) perform optimally and that data remains accessible and protected.

VMware offers various tools and features to manage storage effectively, allowing administrators to allocate, provision, and monitor storage resources seamlessly. One of the key components for managing storage in VMware is the VMware vSphere storage infrastructure.

VMware vSphere provides a comprehensive set of features and capabilities for storage management, including support for different storage protocols and storage area networks (SANs). It enables administrators to connect storage devices to ESXi hosts and allocate storage resources to VMs.

When managing storage in VMware, administrators must consider the storage architecture and design. This includes the selection of storage protocols, such as iSCSI, Fibre Channel, or NFS, based on performance and compatibility requirements.

Storage arrays, including network-attached storage (NAS) and storage area network (SAN) devices, are common choices for VMware environments. These storage solutions offer scalable and high-performance storage options that can meet the demands of virtualized workloads.

Thin provisioning is a storage feature that allows administrators to allocate storage on-demand, ensuring that storage space is only consumed as VMs and applications use it. Thin provisioning helps optimize storage utilization and reduces wasted capacity.

VMware vSAN (Virtual Storage Area Network) is a software-defined storage solution that integrates directly with VMware vSphere. vSAN pools local storage resources from ESXi hosts to create a distributed storage system that is highly scalable and resilient.

Storage profiles in VMware vSphere enable administrators to define and apply specific storage requirements and policies to VMs. These profiles ensure that VMs are provisioned with the appropriate storage resources, such as performance levels and redundancy.

Storage DRS (Distributed Resource Scheduler) is a feature in VMware vSphere that automates the placement and balancing of VMs across storage devices to optimize performance and capacity utilization.

VMware offers support for storage snapshots, which are point-in-time copies of storage volumes. These snapshots serve as backups and can be used for data recovery and testing without impacting the production environment.

Monitoring and performance tuning are essential aspects of managing storage in VMware. Administrators can use monitoring tools and performance metrics to assess storage performance and identify potential bottlenecks or issues.

Storage I/O control is a feature in VMware vSphere that allows administrators to prioritize and allocate storage I/O resources to VMs based on their importance and performance requirements.

Storage vMotion is a feature that enables live migration of VMs between different storage devices or datastores without downtime. This feature is valuable for load balancing and storage maintenance tasks.

VMware Site Recovery Manager (SRM) is a disaster recovery solution that provides automated failover and failback capabilities, ensuring data protection and business continuity in the event of a disaster.

Data deduplication and compression are storage optimization techniques that reduce storage space requirements by eliminating redundant data and compressing data to occupy less space. These techniques help maximize storage efficiency and reduce costs.

Backup and data protection strategies are critical when managing storage in VMware. Regularly backing up VMs and data ensures data availability and recoverability in case of data loss or system failures.

Storage tiering involves categorizing data based on its access patterns and importance. Frequently accessed and critical data can be stored on high-performance storage tiers, while less frequently accessed data can reside on lower-cost storage tiers.

Storage policies and access controls define how storage resources are allocated and accessed by VMs. Implement policies to ensure that VMs receive the appropriate storage resources and that data remains secure and compliant with regulatory requirements.

In summary, managing storage in VMware is a crucial aspect of maintaining a robust and efficient virtualized environment. VMware provides a range of features and tools to allocate, provision, and monitor storage resources effectively. By understanding the principles and capabilities of storage management in VMware, administrators can optimize storage utilization, ensure data protection, and support the performance requirements of virtualized workloads.

Chapter 7: Snapshotting and Cloning Virtual Machines

Using snapshots for virtual machines (VMs) is a valuable technique in virtualization environments, providing a means to capture and preserve the state of a VM at a specific point in time. Snapshots serve as a backup mechanism and offer several benefits for managing and protecting VMs.

When a snapshot is created, it effectively captures a "point-in-time" image of the VM, including its configuration, disk state, and memory contents. This snapshot acts as a reference point that can be used for various purposes, such as recovering from errors, testing software changes, and maintaining historical records.

Snapshots are particularly useful when making changes to a VM, such as installing software updates or performing configuration modifications. Before making these changes, you can create a snapshot to preserve the VM's current state. If the changes cause issues or unexpected behavior, you can revert to the snapshot, effectively "rolling back" the VM to its previous state.

Creating a snapshot is a straightforward process within most virtualization platforms. Typically, you access the VM's management interface, select the VM for which you want to create a snapshot, and initiate the snapshot creation process. Some platforms allow you to name the snapshot and provide a brief description for reference.

Once a snapshot is created, the VM continues to operate normally. Any changes made to the VM, such as file modifications or software installations, are recorded in the snapshot's delta disk, ensuring that the original VM state remains intact.

Snapshots provide an efficient way to test software updates or changes in a controlled environment. By creating a snapshot before implementing changes, you can isolate and evaluate the impact of those changes without affecting the production environment.

Snapshots can also serve as a valuable tool for troubleshooting VM issues. If a VM experiences unexpected behavior or errors, you can revert to a snapshot taken before the issues occurred to identify and isolate the root cause of the problem.

Snapshots are space-efficient because they only store the changes made to the VM's disk since the snapshot was created. This "differencing disk" approach reduces storage requirements compared to creating full copies of the VM. However, it's essential to monitor snapshot disk usage to prevent running out of storage space.

To maintain the efficiency of snapshots, it's advisable to limit the number of snapshots associated with a VM. While multiple snapshots can be created, having too many can lead to increased storage consumption and performance degradation when consolidating snapshots.

Consolidating snapshots is a process that combines the changes from multiple snapshots into a single snapshot or the original VM state. It is essential to periodically consolidate snapshots to maintain efficient storage usage and prevent snapshot chains from becoming excessively long.

Snapshots should not be used as a long-term backup solution. While they provide a point-in-time recovery option, they are not a substitute for regular backups. Over time, snapshot files can grow large, potentially impacting storage performance and availability.

Backups are more suitable for long-term data protection and recovery, as they store VM data in a separate location, ensuring data integrity and availability even if the original VM and its snapshots become inaccessible.

When using snapshots, it's important to have a clear snapshot management strategy. This includes defining policies for snapshot creation, retention, and consolidation based on the specific needs of your virtualization environment.

Snapshot management should also consider the impact of snapshots on VM performance. Excessive snapshot use or maintaining snapshots for extended periods can lead to performance degradation, as VMs must access multiple snapshot layers to retrieve data.

Monitoring snapshot age and usage is essential for effective management. Regularly review and clean up old snapshots that are no longer needed to optimize storage and maintain VM performance.

In summary, using snapshots for virtual machines is a valuable technique that provides a means to capture and preserve the state of a VM at a specific point in time. Snapshots offer benefits for managing, testing, and troubleshooting VMs, but it's crucial to use them judiciously and complement them with a robust backup strategy for long-term data protection and recovery. By understanding how to effectively use and manage snapshots, administrators can leverage this feature to enhance VM management and maintain data integrity in virtualized environments.

Cloning virtual machines is a powerful feature in virtualization that allows you to duplicate an existing virtual machine (VM) to create identical copies for various purposes. Cloning a VM is particularly valuable when you need to deploy multiple VMs with the same configuration or when you want to create a backup or template for future use. There are different types of VM cloning methods available in virtualization platforms, including full clone and linked clone. A full clone creates an independent copy of the original VM, with its own set of virtual disks and resources, making it entirely self-contained. A linked clone, on the other hand, shares virtual disks with the original VM and creates a new VM with a separate configuration and memory state. Linked clones are more space-efficient but rely on the presence of the original VM to function correctly. To initiate the cloning process, access your virtualization platform's management interface and select the VM you want to clone. Specify the type of clone you want to create, either a full clone or a linked clone, based on your requirements and available resources. Give the cloned VM a unique name and define its location or folder within your virtualization environment. You can also customize the cloned VM by specifying hardware configurations, such as CPU, memory, and network settings. Some virtualization platforms offer customization options that allow you to modify settings during the cloning process, such as changing network settings or specifying a different operating system. Cloning a VM typically involves copying the VM's virtual disks, configuration files, and memory state to create the new VM. The process may take some time, depending on the size of the VM and the speed of your storage subsystem. Once the cloning process is complete, you can power on the new VM and start using it just like any other VM in your environment. Cloning VMs is beneficial for various use cases, including:

Development and Testing: Clone VMs to create isolated environments for software development, testing, and quality assurance.

Scaling Applications: Quickly scale applications by creating multiple identical VMs to distribute workloads.

Disaster Recovery: Maintain cloned VMs as backup copies that can be used for disaster recovery in case of VM failures.

Template Creation: Create VM templates with specific configurations and software installations that can be easily deployed when needed.

Replicating Configurations: Duplicate VMs with complex configurations, ensuring consistency across multiple instances. When using linked clones, it's important to understand that they rely on the original VM for shared virtual disks, which means changes made to shared data in the original VM can affect all linked clones. Linked clones are space-efficient as they only consume storage for unique data and rely on the parent VM for shared data blocks. To maintain data consistency and isolation between linked clones, consider using features like VMware's "VMware Tools Synchronization" or similar mechanisms in other virtualization platforms. Regularly monitor and manage cloned VMs to ensure they remain up-to-date with software updates, security patches, and configurations. Document the purpose and use of each cloned VM to track their roles and functionalities within your virtualization environment. Additionally, consider implementing automation and orchestration tools to streamline the cloning process and maintain consistency in your virtual machine deployments. In summary, cloning virtual machines is a powerful capability in virtualization that allows you to duplicate VMs for various purposes, such as development, testing, scaling applications, disaster recovery, and template creation. Understanding the different types of cloning methods and their implications is essential for effectively using this feature in your virtualization environment. By leveraging VM cloning, you can improve operational efficiency, enhance scalability, and ensure data consistency across your virtualized infrastructure.

Chapter 8: Backup and Recovery in VMware

VMware backup essentials are crucial components of any virtualization strategy, ensuring the protection, availability, and recoverability of virtual machines (VMs) and their data. Effective VMware backup solutions help organizations safeguard their virtualized workloads, applications, and critical data against various risks, including hardware failures, data corruption, human errors, and disasters. VMware environments are inherently complex, with multiple VMs running on shared physical hardware, making it essential to have a robust backup strategy in place. Backup solutions designed for VMware offer several key features and benefits that address the unique challenges posed by virtualization. One of the primary features of VMware backup solutions is the ability to perform agentless backups. Agentless backups do not require the installation of backup agents within each VM, simplifying backup management and reducing resource overhead. Instead, VMware backup solutions leverage VMware's vStorage API for Data Protection (VADP) to interact with VMs and their data directly. VMware VADP provides efficient and consistent backup and recovery operations, including features like Changed Block Tracking (CBT) for incremental backups. Incremental backups only capture and store the changed data blocks since the last backup, minimizing backup windows and storage requirements. Backup solutions for VMware also offer granular recovery options, allowing administrators to restore individual files, folders, or even application items from within VM backups. This granular recovery capability is particularly valuable when retrieving specific data without the need for full VM restores. VMware backup solutions support both image-level and application-aware backups. Image-level backups capture the entire VM, including its configuration, virtual disks, and memory state. Application-aware backups, on the other hand, ensure consistency by quiescing applications during backup, allowing for application-level recovery. Consistency is crucial for applications like databases, email servers, and other mission-critical services. VMware backup solutions offer various backup storage options, including local storage, network-attached storage (NAS), and storage area networks (SANs). These flexible storage choices enable organizations to tailor their backup storage to their specific requirements and budget constraints. Off-site backup and replication are essential components of VMware backup strategies. Off-site backups provide an additional layer of data protection, ensuring data recoverability in case of on-site disasters or hardware failures. Replication allows organizations to maintain real-time copies of VMs at remote locations for disaster recovery purposes. Backup solutions for VMware often include deduplication and compression technologies, which optimize storage utilization by reducing redundant data and compressing backup files. These technologies help organizations reduce storage costs and minimize the impact of backups on their infrastructure. VMware backup solutions also provide scheduling and automation features that allow administrators to define backup policies, set retention periods, and automate backup processes. Automation streamlines backup operations and ensures that critical VMs are backed up on schedule. Monitoring and reporting capabilities are integral to VMware backup solutions, offering insights into backup job status, success rates, and storage utilization. This visibility helps administrators proactively address any issues and ensures that backup and recovery operations are running smoothly. Security features, including data encryption and access controls, protect VM backups from unauthorized access and data breaches. Data encryption ensures that backup data remains confidential, while access controls restrict who can perform backup and recovery tasks. Testing and verification features in VMware backup solutions enable administrators to validate the recoverability of VM backups through automated testing processes. This verification helps organizations have confidence in their ability to restore VMs and data when needed. Retention policies in VMware backup solutions allow organizations to define how long backups are retained, ensuring compliance with data retention and regulatory requirements. Retention policies also help manage storage costs by automatically deleting older backups that are no longer needed. When selecting a VMware backup solution, organizations should consider factors such as scalability, ease of management, integration with existing infrastructure, and support for different backup targets. Scalability ensures that the backup solution can grow with the organization's evolving virtualization needs. Ease of management simplifies backup operations and reduces administrative overhead. Integration with existing infrastructure ensures a seamless backup process and minimizes disruptions. Support for different backup targets provides flexibility in choosing the most suitable storage options. A well-planned VMware backup strategy is essential for protecting the investments made in virtualization technology and ensuring business continuity. By leveraging VMware backup essentials, organizations can mitigate risks, improve data availability, and confidently navigate the complexities of virtualized environments. Effective VMware backup solutions offer a comprehensive set of features and capabilities that cater to the unique challenges of virtualization, ensuring the resilience and recoverability of VMs and their data. Strategies for VMware backup and recovery are essential components of a comprehensive data protection plan in virtualized environments. Effective backup and recovery strategies ensure that virtual machines (VMs) and their data remain available and recoverable in the event of hardware failures, data corruption, human errors, or disasters. VMware environments present unique challenges, such as the dynamic nature of VMs, shared storage resources, and the need to maintain data consistency. To address these challenges, organizations should implement strategies that encompass several key principles. First and foremost, organizations must define their recovery objectives, including recovery time objectives (RTOs) and recovery point objectives (RPOs). RTOs specify the maximum acceptable downtime for VMs and applications, while RPOs define how much data loss is acceptable in case of a failure. These objectives guide the selection of backup and recovery solutions and influence the design of backup and replication processes. Implementing a combination of full backups and incremental backups is a common strategy for VMware environments. Full backups capture the entire VM, providing a complete image that can be used for full VM restores. Incremental backups, on the other hand, capture only the changes made to VMs since the last backup, reducing backup windows and storage requirements. By using both types of backups, organizations can balance data protection and resource efficiency. Backup frequency should align with RPOs, ensuring that backups occur frequently enough to meet recovery objectives. Regularly scheduled backups help capture changes to VMs and applications, minimizing data loss in case of a failure. Organizations should consider the use of backup storage targets, such as network-attached storage (NAS), storage area networks (SANs), or cloud-based storage. These targets offer flexibility and scalability while providing a secure and off-site location for backup data. Implementing a tiered backup storage strategy allows organizations to optimize cost and performance by using different storage types for backups. For example, high-performance storage may be used for recent backups, while lower-cost, long-term storage can store older backups. In addition to traditional backup, organizations should consider replication as part of their recovery strategy. Replication maintains real-time copies of VMs at remote locations, providing a near-instantaneous recovery option in case of a disaster or hardware failure. Replication solutions are especially valuable for critical applications and VMs that require minimal downtime. Testing and validation of backup and recovery processes are critical components of a successful strategy. Organizations should regularly perform recovery tests to ensure that backups are valid and can be successfully restored. Automated recovery testing tools can help streamline this process and verify the recoverability of VMs and data. Retention policies play a vital role in managing backup data. Organizations should establish policies that define how long backups are retained based on regulatory requirements, business needs, and available storage resources. Retention policies help manage storage costs and ensure compliance with data retention regulations. Security measures, such as data encryption and access controls, protect backup data from unauthorized access and data breaches. Encryption ensures that backup data remains confidential and secure, while access controls restrict who can perform backup and recovery tasks. Monitoring and reporting tools provide visibility into the status and performance of backup and recovery operations. These tools help administrators proactively identify issues, ensure compliance with backup policies, and optimize backup processes. Integration with existing infrastructure is essential to ensure a seamless backup and recovery process. Organizations should select backup solutions that integrate well with their virtualization platform, storage infrastructure, and management tools. Automation and orchestration capabilities enhance the efficiency and reliability of backup and recovery processes. Automating routine tasks, such as backup job scheduling and testing, reduces the risk of human errors and ensures consistency in backup operations. Orchestration tools help automate complex recovery workflows, ensuring that VMs and applications are recovered in the correct order and according to business priorities. Regularly reviewing and updating backup and recovery strategies is crucial to adapt to changing business needs and technological advancements. Organizations should conduct periodic assessments to evaluate the effectiveness of their strategies, identify areas for improvement, and ensure alignment with recovery objectives. In summary, strategies for VMware backup and recovery are critical components of a comprehensive data protection plan in virtualized environments. These strategies encompass principles such as defining recovery objectives, using a combination of backup types, selecting appropriate storage targets, and implementing testing and validation processes. By following these principles and considering factors like retention policies, security measures, and integration with existing infrastructure, organizations can build robust VMware backup and recovery strategies that ensure data availability and recoverability while minimizing downtime and data loss in virtualized environments.

Chapter 9: Exploring Advanced VMware Features

An advanced features overview provides insights into the advanced capabilities and functionalities offered by virtualization platforms, enhancing the management and optimization of virtualized environments. These advanced features are designed to address complex scenarios and requirements, providing administrators with greater control and flexibility. One such advanced feature is live migration, which allows for the seamless movement of virtual machines (VMs) from one physical host to another without interrupting their operation. Live migration is particularly valuable for load balancing, hardware maintenance, and ensuring high availability. Storage vMotion is an extension of live migration that enables the migration of VMs and their associated virtual disks between different datastores while the VMs are running. This feature facilitates storage maintenance, performance optimization, and storage capacity management. Another advanced feature is fault tolerance, which provides continuous availability for VMs by creating a real-time duplicate VM on a separate host. In the event of a hardware failure, the duplicate VM seamlessly takes over, eliminating downtime and data loss. Distributed Resource Scheduler (DRS) is an advanced feature that automatically balances VM workloads across physical hosts in a cluster. DRS considers factors such as CPU and memory utilization, ensuring optimal resource allocation and performance. Resource Pools allow administrators to allocate CPU and memory resources to groups of VMs, ensuring that critical workloads receive the necessary resources while preventing resource contention. High Availability (HA) is an advanced feature that automatically restarts VMs on available hosts in the event of a host failure, minimizing downtime. Network and storage I/O control are advanced features that enable administrators to prioritize and allocate network and storage resources to VMs based on their importance and performance requirements. VMware Distributed Switch (vDS) is an advanced networking feature that provides centralized management and monitoring of network configurations across multiple hosts in a cluster. vDS enhances network scalability, security, and consistency. Virtual Distributed Port Groups within vDS allow for the grouping and management of network ports, simplifying network configuration and maintenance. Network redundancy and failover capabilities are advanced features that ensure network connectivity remains available in case of network adapter or switch failures. Storage APIs, such as VMware vStorage APIs for Array Integration (VAAI) and vStorage APIs for Storage Awareness (VASA), allow virtualization platforms to offload storage operations to compatible storage arrays, enhancing performance and efficiency. Storage I/O control and quality of service (QoS) features enable administrators to manage and prioritize storage resources for VMs, ensuring consistent performance. Virtual machine snapshots, an advanced feature, capture the state of a VM at a specific point in time, allowing for easy recovery and testing. Distributed Switch Port Mirroring is an advanced network monitoring feature that captures network traffic from multiple VMs and forwards it to a designated network analyzer for analysis. Virtual Security Appliances (VSAs) are advanced security features that provide network security and firewall capabilities within the virtualization infrastructure. Host Profiles are an advanced configuration management feature that enables administrators to maintain consistent host configurations across a cluster, ensuring compliance and simplifying host deployment. Advanced features also encompass virtualization management tools and interfaces, such as VMware vCenter Server and vCenter Orchestrator, which provide centralized management, automation, and orchestration capabilities. vCenter Server enables administrators to manage multiple hosts and clusters from a single interface, streamlining administrative tasks. vCenter Orchestrator automates complex workflows and processes, enhancing operational efficiency and reducing manual intervention. Advanced backup and recovery solutions, such as VMware Site Recovery Manager (SRM), offer automated disaster recovery and failover capabilities, ensuring business continuity in case of disasters. Software-defined networking (SDN) and network virtualization are advanced features that abstract network services and configurations from the underlying hardware, enabling greater flexibility and agility in network management. Hybrid cloud integration is an advanced feature that allows organizations to seamlessly extend their virtualized environments to public or private cloud platforms, providing scalability and flexibility. Advanced features also encompass security enhancements, such as virtual machine encryption, secure boot, and virtual Trusted Platform Module (vTPM), which protect VMs and data from security threats. Advanced performance monitoring and analytics tools provide insights into the performance and health of virtualized environments, enabling proactive issue identification and resolution. These advanced features collectively empower organizations to build and manage resilient, efficient, and scalable virtualized environments. By leveraging these capabilities, administrators can address complex requirements, optimize resource utilization, enhance security, and ensure high availability for critical workloads. Understanding and effectively utilizing advanced features are essential for maximizing the benefits of virtualization and meeting the evolving needs of modern IT environments.

Performance optimization is a critical aspect of managing virtualized environments, and advanced features play a crucial role in achieving optimal performance. These advanced features provide administrators with the tools and capabilities needed to fine-tune virtualized infrastructure for efficiency and responsiveness. One such feature is Distributed Resource Scheduler (DRS), which intelligently balances VM workloads across physical hosts in a cluster, optimizing resource utilization and ensuring consistent performance. DRS considers factors like CPU and memory usage, making real-time recommendations for VM migrations to maintain a balanced environment. Resource Pools are another advanced feature that allows administrators to allocate CPU and memory resources to groups of VMs based on their importance and resource requirements. This granular control ensures that critical workloads receive the necessary resources while preventing resource contention and ensuring optimal performance. High Availability (HA) is a critical advanced feature that automatically restarts VMs on available hosts in the event of a host failure, minimizing downtime and ensuring uninterrupted service. Network and storage I/O control features enable administrators to prioritize and allocate network and storage resources to VMs based on their performance requirements. By ensuring that critical VMs receive the necessary resources, these features enhance overall system responsiveness. Storage I/O control also includes features like Quality of Service (QoS) that help manage and prioritize storage resources for VMs, ensuring consistent storage performance. VMware Distributed Switch (vDS) is an advanced networking feature that provides centralized management and monitoring of network configurations across multiple hosts in a cluster. vDS enhances network scalability, security, and consistency, contributing to improved performance. Within vDS, Virtual Distributed Port Groups allow for the grouping and management of network ports, simplifying network configuration and maintenance. Network redundancy and failover capabilities, another advanced feature, ensure that network connectivity remains available in case of network adapter or switch failures, enhancing network reliability and performance. Storage APIs, such as VMware vStorage APIs for Array Integration (VAAI) and vStorage APIs for Storage Awareness (VASA), offload storage operations to compatible storage arrays, improving storage performance and efficiency. These APIs allow virtualization platforms to leverage hardware acceleration for tasks like copying and cloning VMs, enhancing performance. Virtual machine snapshots, an advanced feature, provide a way to capture the state of a VM at a specific point in time, allowing for easy recovery and testing without affecting the VM's ongoing operation. Distributed Switch Port Mirroring is an advanced network monitoring feature that captures network traffic from multiple VMs and forwards it to a designated network analyzer for analysis, aiding in performance troubleshooting. Virtual Security Appliances (VSAs) are advanced security features that provide network security and firewall capabilities within the virtualization infrastructure, enhancing security without compromising performance. Host Profiles are an advanced configuration management feature that ensures consistent host configurations across a cluster, simplifying host deployment and reducing configuration errors that could impact performance. Advanced backup and recovery solutions, such as VMware Site Recovery Manager (SRM), offer automated disaster recovery and failover capabilities, minimizing downtime and ensuring business continuity in the face of disasters. Performance monitoring and analytics tools are advanced features that provide insights into the performance and health of virtualized environments, enabling proactive issue identification and resolution. These tools help administrators optimize resource usage, troubleshoot performance bottlenecks, and ensure that VMs meet their performance requirements. Software-defined networking (SDN) and network virtualization are advanced features that abstract network services and configurations from the underlying hardware, enabling greater flexibility and agility in network management, which can enhance performance and responsiveness. Hybrid cloud integration is an advanced feature that allows organizations to seamlessly extend their virtualized environments to public or private cloud platforms, providing scalability and flexibility to meet changing performance demands. Advanced features also encompass security enhancements, such as virtual machine encryption, secure boot, and virtual Trusted Platform Module (vTPM), which protect VMs and data from security threats without sacrificing performance. Advanced performance optimization techniques, such as CPU and memory overcommitment, can help organizations maximize resource utilization and performance while ensuring responsiveness. CPU overcommitment allows for the allocation of more virtual CPU cores to VMs than there are physical CPU cores, provided that the average CPU usage remains within acceptable levels. Memory overcommitment, similarly, allows for the allocation of more virtual memory to VMs than there is physical memory, relying on techniques like transparent page sharing to minimize memory usage. However, administrators must carefully monitor and manage overcommitted resources to avoid performance degradation. Advanced features collectively empower administrators to fine-tune virtualized infrastructure for optimal performance, ensuring that VM workloads run efficiently and responsively. These features enhance resource utilization, minimize downtime, improve network and storage performance, and provide tools for proactive performance monitoring and troubleshooting. Understanding and effectively utilizing advanced features are essential for achieving and maintaining peak performance in virtualized environments, meeting the performance demands of modern IT workloads, and delivering optimal user experiences.

Chapter 10: Troubleshooting Common Issues in VMware

Common VMware issues can impact the stability and performance of virtualized environments, requiring prompt identification and resolution to maintain smooth operations. One common issue is resource contention, where multiple virtual machines (VMs) compete for CPU, memory, or storage resources, resulting in degraded performance for some VMs. Resource contention can lead to slow response times, application errors, and decreased overall efficiency. To address this issue, administrators can use performance monitoring tools to identify resource bottlenecks and reallocate resources as needed. Another frequent problem is snapshot sprawl, which occurs when multiple snapshots are created for VMs but not properly managed or cleaned up over time. Snapshot sprawl can consume excessive storage space and impact VM performance. To mitigate this issue, administrators should establish snapshot management policies and regularly consolidate or delete unnecessary snapshots. Network connectivity problems are also common in VMware environments, affecting communication between VMs or between VMs and external networks. Issues like misconfigured network settings, firewall rules, or network adapter failures can disrupt connectivity. Administrators should conduct thorough network troubleshooting, validate configurations, and ensure proper network connectivity for VMs. Storage-related issues often arise due to factors like disk space exhaustion, storage array failures, or performance bottlenecks. When VMs run out of disk space, they may become unresponsive or fail to function correctly. To address storage problems, administrators should monitor storage capacity, implement efficient storage management practices, and ensure redundancy and failover mechanisms are in place. VMware tools and services can sometimes experience problems, impacting the management and operation of VMs. Issues with services like vCenter Server or ESXi hosts can lead to VM performance degradation or unavailability. Administrators should regularly update VMware components, apply patches, and maintain service health to prevent such problems. Compatibility issues can occur when VMs are moved or migrated between different VMware products or versions. Compatibility problems may arise when older VMs are run on newer VMware software or when VMs are moved between different hypervisors. Administrators should assess compatibility before performing migrations or upgrades to prevent issues. Performance bottlenecks are common, causing VMs to operate slower than expected. Bottlenecks can occur in CPU, memory, storage, or network resources, affecting VM responsiveness. Administrators should use performance monitoring and analysis tools to identify and address performance bottlenecks proactively. Security vulnerabilities are a significant concern in virtualized environments, as any breach can impact multiple VMs. Common security issues include unpatched VMs, misconfigured security settings, and inadequate access controls. Administrators should regularly update VMs, implement security best practices, and conduct security audits to minimize vulnerabilities. Backup and recovery issues can lead to data loss or extended downtime in the event of a failure. Problems like incomplete backups, slow restores, or backup storage limitations can hinder data protection. Administrators should regularly test backups, optimize backup strategies, and ensure reliable recovery processes. Licensing and compliance issues can arise when organizations fail to properly manage their VMware licenses or comply with licensing terms. Improper licensing can lead to unexpected costs or legal consequences. Administrators should maintain accurate license records and ensure compliance with VMware licensing agreements. Storage performance issues can negatively impact VM operations, causing slow disk access or data unavailability. Factors like storage latency, I/O bottlenecks, or misconfigured storage settings can contribute to storage performance problems. Administrators should monitor storage performance, optimize storage configurations, and address underlying storage infrastructure issues. Virtual machine sprawl occurs when organizations create numerous VMs without adequate management or oversight. Excessive VMs can consume resources, complicate management, and increase costs. Administrators should implement VM lifecycle management practices, including provisioning, tracking, and decommissioning, to control VM sprawl. Failure to plan for high availability can result in unplanned downtime during hardware failures or other unexpected events. VMware provides features like High Availability (HA) and Fault Tolerance (FT) to address these concerns. Administrators should design and configure HA and FT solutions to meet availability requirements and minimize downtime. In summary, common VMware issues can impact the performance, availability, and security of virtualized environments. Administrators should be prepared to address resource contention, snapshot sprawl, network connectivity problems, storage issues, service disruptions, compatibility challenges, performance bottlenecks, security vulnerabilities, backup and recovery problems, licensing and compliance issues, storage performance concerns, virtual machine sprawl, and high availability planning. Proactive monitoring, regular maintenance, and effective troubleshooting are essential for maintaining the health and reliability of VMware environments. By addressing these common issues and implementing best practices, organizations can maximize the benefits of virtualization while minimizing disruptions and risks.

Troubleshooting virtualization problems is a critical skill for administrators to ensure the smooth operation of virtualized environments. When issues arise, it's essential to diagnose and resolve them promptly to minimize downtime and maintain the integrity of the virtual infrastructure. One common problem that administrators may encounter is virtual machine (VM) performance degradation, where VMs become slow or unresponsive. This issue can occur due to resource contention, such as CPU or memory shortages, or underlying storage problems. To troubleshoot performance degradation, administrators should use performance monitoring tools to identify the root cause and reallocate resources if necessary. Network connectivity problems can disrupt communication between VMs or between VMs and external networks, impacting the functionality of applications and services. Troubleshooting network issues involves verifying network configurations, checking firewall rules, and ensuring that network adapters are functioning correctly. Storage-related problems can result in VMs experiencing disk-related errors, slow disk access, or data corruption. Troubleshooting storage issues may involve monitoring storage capacity, verifying storage array health, and addressing storage latency or I/O bottlenecks. VMware tools and services may encounter issues that affect the management and operation of VMs. Problems with services like vCenter Server or ESXi hosts can lead to VM unavailability or performance problems. Administrators should check service health, apply patches, and perform regular maintenance to prevent these issues. Compatibility problems can arise when VMs are moved between different VMware products or versions, leading to compatibility-related errors or unexpected behavior. Troubleshooting compatibility issues involves assessing compatibility before migrations or upgrades and ensuring that software versions align. Performance bottlenecks can cause VMs to operate at reduced performance levels, affecting user experience and application responsiveness. Troubleshooting performance bottlenecks requires analyzing performance data, identifying resource constraints, and optimizing resource allocation. Security vulnerabilities can expose VMs to potential threats or breaches, compromising data and system integrity. Troubleshooting security issues entails patching VMs, implementing security best practices, and conducting regular security audits. Backup and recovery problems can hinder data protection and disaster recovery efforts, resulting in data loss or extended downtime. Troubleshooting backup and recovery issues involves testing backups, optimizing backup strategies, and ensuring reliable recovery processes. Licensing and compliance issues can have financial and legal consequences if not managed properly. Troubleshooting licensing and compliance issues requires maintaining accurate license records and adhering to licensing agreements. Storage performance issues can negatively impact VM operations, causing slow disk access or data unavailability. Troubleshooting storage performance problems entails monitoring storage performance metrics, optimizing storage configurations, and addressing underlying storage infrastructure issues. Virtual machine sprawl occurs when organizations create numerous VMs without adequate management or oversight. Troubleshooting VM sprawl involves implementing VM lifecycle management practices to control and manage VMs effectively. Failure to plan for high availability can result in unplanned downtime during hardware failures or unexpected events. Troubleshooting high availability issues requires designing and configuring high availability solutions to meet availability requirements. In summary, troubleshooting virtualization problems is a crucial skill for administrators to maintain the performance, availability, and security of virtualized environments. Common issues include VM performance degradation, network connectivity problems, storage-related problems, service disruptions, compatibility challenges, performance bottlenecks, security vulnerabilities, backup and recovery issues, licensing and compliance concerns, storage performance problems, virtual machine sprawl, and high availability planning. Proactive monitoring, regular maintenance, and effective troubleshooting are essential for ensuring the health and reliability of virtualized environments. By addressing these common issues and implementing best practices, organizations can maximize the benefits of virtualization while minimizing disruptions and risks.

BOOK 2
MASTERING VIRTUALBOX
BUILDING AND MANAGING VIRTUAL ENVIRONMENTS

ROB BOTWRIGHT

Chapter 1: Introduction to VirtualBox

Virtualization with VirtualBox is a powerful technology that enables users to run multiple operating systems on a single physical machine. This technology has revolutionized the way we use computers, allowing for greater flexibility, efficiency, and resource utilization. At its core, virtualization is the process of creating virtual instances of computer hardware, including processors, memory, storage, and network interfaces, to run multiple operating systems concurrently. Virtualization technology is widely used in both enterprise and personal computing environments, offering numerous benefits and use cases. One of the primary advantages of virtualization is the ability to consolidate multiple physical servers or desktops onto a single physical host, reducing hardware costs and simplifying management. With VirtualBox, you can create and manage these virtual environments with ease. VirtualBox is a free, open-source virtualization platform developed by Oracle, designed to be both powerful and user-friendly. It supports a wide range of guest operating systems, including various flavors of Windows, Linux distributions, macOS, and more. VirtualBox is compatible with various host operating systems, such as Windows, macOS, Linux, and Solaris, making it a versatile choice for virtualization needs. VirtualBox provides a host of features that cater to the needs of both beginners and experienced users. For those new to virtualization, it offers a straightforward and intuitive graphical user interface (GUI) that simplifies the process of creating and managing virtual machines (VMs). With just a few clicks, users can create a new VM, install an operating system, and start running applications within the virtual environment. VirtualBox also offers snapshot functionality, allowing users to save the current state of a VM and return to it later, providing an essential safety net for experimenting or troubleshooting. For more advanced users, VirtualBox offers command-line interfaces and scripting options for automation and customization. VirtualBox supports various virtualization techniques, including hardware-assisted virtualization (Intel VT-x and AMD-V) and software-based virtualization. This flexibility ensures that VirtualBox can run on a wide range of host systems, from older hardware to modern, high-performance machines. Virtual machines created with VirtualBox can be easily transported and shared between different hosts, making it a versatile solution for development, testing, and demonstrations. The ability to run multiple operating systems on a single host is invaluable for various scenarios. For instance, software developers often use virtualization to create isolated development and testing environments. By running different operating systems in VMs, developers can ensure that their software works seamlessly across various platforms and configurations. IT professionals also benefit from virtualization when setting up test environments to evaluate new software or configurations without impacting production systems. Virtualization is a crucial technology in the realm of server consolidation. In data centers, it enables organizations to reduce the number of physical servers, resulting in cost savings, lower energy consumption, and easier management. Virtualization also plays a pivotal role in disaster recovery and business continuity planning. By maintaining offsite backups of virtual machines, organizations can quickly recover from hardware failures or unforeseen disasters. VirtualBox, with its portability and snapshot features, contributes to these disaster recovery strategies. The concept of virtualization extends beyond server environments. On desktop or personal computing systems, users can employ virtualization to run multiple operating systems side by side. For example, a Windows user might run a Linux VM for development work or testing, or a macOS user might run Windows applications within a virtual environment. This flexibility allows users to leverage the strengths of different operating systems while maintaining a single physical machine. Virtualization can also be used to isolate potentially risky tasks, such as browsing untrusted websites or testing software with unknown security implications. By doing so within a VM, users can protect their host operating system and data from potential threats. VirtualBox provides features like snapshotting and cloning to facilitate these isolation scenarios. In the context of VirtualBox, a virtual machine (VM) is a self-contained instance of an operating system running within a virtualized environment. Each VM operates independently, with its own resources and configuration settings. Users can create, modify, and delete VMs as needed, tailoring them to specific tasks or purposes. Within a VM, users can install and run software, browse the web, access files, and perform various computing tasks, just as they would on a physical machine. However, the underlying hardware resources are shared among multiple VMs, with the hypervisor (in this case, VirtualBox) managing resource allocation and isolation. VirtualBox allows users to customize the hardware configuration of each VM to meet specific requirements. For instance, users can allocate a certain amount of memory, CPU cores, and storage space to each VM, tailoring the resources to the workload. Users can also configure virtual network adapters to enable communication between VMs and the host or between VMs themselves. Additionally, VirtualBox supports various storage options, including virtual hard disks (VHDs), which are files that represent the VM's storage, and physical partitions or drives passed through to the VM. Installing an operating system within a VirtualBox VM is a straightforward process. Users typically begin by creating a new VM and specifying its properties, such as the type and version of the guest operating system, the amount of memory, and the number of CPU cores allocated. Once the VM is configured, users can attach an installation ISO image or physical installation media to the VM's virtual optical drive. Upon starting the VM, it boots from the chosen installation media, allowing users to follow the standard installation procedures for the guest operating system. After the operating system is installed, users can customize and configure it as needed, just as they would on a physical machine. VirtualBox provides a range of tools and utilities to enhance the functionality of VMs. For example, users can install VirtualBox Guest Additions within the guest operating system to improve integration between the guest and host. Guest Additions provide features like shared clipboard, seamless mouse integration, and enhanced display resolution. VirtualBox also supports a variety of virtual disk formats, making it compatible with other virtualization platforms. Users can import or export VMs in formats such as VirtualBox's Virtual Disk Image (VDI), VMware's Virtual Machine Disk (VMDK), or Microsoft's Virtual Hard Disk (VHD). This flexibility ensures that VMs created with VirtualBox can be easily migrated or shared across different virtualization environments. In addition to the graphical user interface (GUI), VirtualBox offers command-line interfaces (CLIs) for managing VMs and performing advanced tasks. These CLIs provide scripting capabilities for automation and integration with other tools and systems. Administrators and power users often leverage the command-line options to automate repetitive tasks or customize VM configurations. VirtualBox also supports remote management through the VirtualBox Remote Desktop Protocol (VRDP), allowing users to access VMs remotely. Additionally, VirtualBox includes a snapshot feature that allows users to capture the current state of a VM, including its memory and storage contents. Snapshots serve as restore points, enabling users to revert a VM to a previous state quickly. This feature is invaluable for testing, development, and troubleshooting scenarios, as it provides a safety net for experimentation. Cloning is another useful feature in VirtualBox, allowing users to create duplicate copies of VMs. Cloning is particularly beneficial when setting up multiple VMs with identical configurations or when creating templates for consistent VM deployments. VirtualBox's extensibility is another notable aspect of the platform. Through the use of extensions and third-party plugins, users can enhance VirtualBox's functionality. For example, VirtualBox Extension Packs provide additional features such as USB 2.0 and 3.0 support, VirtualBox Remote Desktop Protocol (VRDP) authentication, and more. These extension packs are easy to install and can significantly extend VirtualBox's capabilities. VirtualBox is continually updated and improved by Oracle and the open-source community. Updates may include bug fixes, performance enhancements, and new features. Users should regularly check for updates and apply them to ensure that they have the latest features and security fixes. In summary, VirtualBox is a versatile and powerful virtualization platform that enables users to run multiple operating systems on a single physical machine. Understanding the principles and features of VirtualBox is essential for harnessing the full potential of virtualization technology. Whether you are a software developer, IT professional, or a tech-savvy user, VirtualBox provides the tools and flexibility to create, manage, and utilize virtual machines effectively. By exploring the capabilities of VirtualBox and its various use cases, you can leverage virtualization to improve efficiency, reduce costs, and enhance your computing experience.

VirtualBox offers a wide range of use cases and benefits that make it a valuable tool in various computing environments. One of the primary use cases of VirtualBox is software development and testing. Developers can create virtual machines (VMs) with different operating systems and configurations to test their software on a variety of platforms. This allows for thorough testing and ensures that applications are compatible across different environments. VirtualBox is also commonly used for creating development environments that mirror production systems, enabling developers to work on projects without impacting the production environment. Another important use case is education and training.

VirtualBox provides a safe and isolated environment for learning about different operating systems, networking concepts, and software installations. Educational institutions often use VirtualBox to create virtual labs where students can practice hands-on exercises and gain practical experience. VirtualBox is an ideal tool for students and instructors alike, as it eliminates the need for dedicated hardware and allows for quick setup and experimentation. IT professionals use VirtualBox for various tasks, such as system administration, server provisioning, and network testing. Administrators can create VMs to simulate network topologies, test server configurations, and evaluate software updates before deploying them in production environments. This reduces the risk of disruptions and ensures that changes will work as intended. VirtualBox's ability to take snapshots of VMs also comes in handy during system administration, as it provides a safety net for system changes. Virtualization is an essential component of cloud computing, and VirtualBox can be used to create private cloud environments for testing and development. Organizations can build their own cloud infrastructure within VirtualBox, allowing them to evaluate cloud technologies, develop cloud-native applications, and test cloud-based services. This provides a cost-effective way to explore cloud computing without relying on external cloud providers. For security professionals, VirtualBox serves as a valuable tool for testing and evaluating security solutions. Penetration testers can create isolated environments to simulate network attacks and vulnerabilities. Security analysts can use VirtualBox to analyze malware samples and conduct forensics investigations without risking the integrity of their host systems. This ability to isolate potentially malicious activities is crucial for maintaining a secure computing environment. VirtualBox supports the concept of sandboxes, where untrusted or potentially harmful software can be run in isolated VMs. This is especially useful for browsing the web or opening email attachments that may contain malware. If the sandboxed environment is compromised, it does not affect the host system, ensuring the security of personal and corporate data. Another significant use case is virtual appliance development. Virtual appliances are pre-configured VMs with specific software applications or services. Developers and system administrators can create virtual appliances for various purposes, such as web servers, databases, content management systems, and more. These appliances can be distributed to end-users or deployed within organizations to streamline software deployment and reduce setup time. VirtualBox's compatibility with the Open Virtualization Format (OVF) standard makes it easy to import and export virtual appliances between different virtualization platforms. One of the notable benefits of using VirtualBox is its cost-effectiveness. As an open-source virtualization platform, VirtualBox is available for free, which makes it an attractive option for organizations and individuals seeking to reduce infrastructure costs. It eliminates the need to invest in expensive virtualization solutions, making it accessible to a wide range of users. VirtualBox's cross-platform compatibility is another significant advantage. It runs on various host operating systems, including Windows, macOS, Linux, and Solaris, making it versatile and adaptable to different environments. Users can create VMs on one host and run them on another, providing flexibility and portability. VirtualBox also supports a wide range of guest operating systems, allowing users to experiment with different platforms and configurations. Another benefit of VirtualBox is its ease of use. The graphical user interface (GUI) provides a straightforward and intuitive way to create, manage, and configure VMs. Users can quickly set up virtual machines, install guest operating systems, and manage snapshots without requiring advanced technical skills. This user-friendly approach makes VirtualBox accessible to both beginners and experienced users. Performance is a crucial consideration in virtualization, and VirtualBox offers various features to optimize performance. It supports hardware-assisted virtualization (Intel VT-x and AMD-V) to improve VM performance by leveraging hardware capabilities. VirtualBox also provides options to allocate CPU cores, memory, and virtual graphics adapters to VMs, allowing users to fine-tune performance settings. Additionally, VirtualBox Guest Additions enhance the integration between host and guest operating systems, providing features like shared clipboard, seamless mouse integration, and enhanced display resolution. Resource management is another advantage of VirtualBox. Administrators can allocate specific amounts of CPU, memory, and storage to each VM, ensuring that resources are distributed efficiently and fairly. This granular control over resource allocation helps prevent resource contention and ensures optimal VM performance. VirtualBox also supports dynamic memory allocation, which allows VMs to use memory more efficiently by allocating memory on-demand based on workload requirements. Storage flexibility is another benefit, as VirtualBox supports various storage options, including virtual hard disks (VHDs), virtual solid-state drives (VSSDs), and the ability to pass through physical partitions or drives to VMs. This versatility allows users to choose the most suitable storage configuration for their workloads. The snapshot and cloning features in VirtualBox provide users with powerful tools for managing VMs. Snapshots capture the current state of a VM, including memory and storage contents, allowing users to return to that state at any time. This is useful for testing, development, and troubleshooting, as it provides a safety net for experimentation. Cloning allows users to create duplicate copies of VMs, simplifying the deployment of multiple VMs with identical configurations. VirtualBox's extensibility is another notable advantage. Users can extend its functionality through the use of extensions and third-party plugins. VirtualBox Extension Packs provide additional features such as USB 2.0 and 3.0 support, VirtualBox Remote Desktop Protocol (VRDP) authentication, and more. These extension packs are easy to install and can significantly enhance VirtualBox's capabilities. Updates and community support are crucial aspects of VirtualBox's benefits. The platform is actively maintained by Oracle and the open-source community, ensuring that it receives regular updates, bug fixes, and performance enhancements. Users can also find a wealth of resources, documentation, and forums online to seek assistance, share knowledge, and troubleshoot issues. In summary, VirtualBox offers a wide range of use cases and benefits that cater to the needs of developers, IT professionals, educators, security experts, and more. Its versatility, cost-effectiveness, cross-platform compatibility, ease of use, performance optimization, resource management, storage flexibility, snapshot and cloning features, extensibility, and community support make it a valuable virtualization tool. Whether you are testing software, learning about different operating systems, securing your computing environment, or optimizing resource usage, VirtualBox provides the tools and capabilities to meet your virtualization needs effectively.

Chapter 2: Installing VirtualBox and Guest Additions

Before you can install VirtualBox on your computer, it's essential to prepare your system adequately to ensure a smooth and trouble-free installation process. First, you should check the system requirements for VirtualBox to confirm that your computer meets the necessary criteria. These requirements typically include specific hardware specifications and supported host operating systems. By verifying your system's compatibility, you can avoid potential installation issues. Next, it's advisable to update your host operating system to the latest available version. Keeping your operating system up-to-date helps ensure that you have the latest security patches, bug fixes, and drivers. This is particularly important for a stable and secure VirtualBox installation. If your host operating system is not up to date, you may encounter compatibility problems or performance issues during installation and usage. Before proceeding with the installation, it's crucial to back up any important data and files on your computer. While VirtualBox itself is not likely to cause data loss, there's always a small risk when making system changes. Creating a backup provides peace of mind and ensures that you can recover your data in case anything goes wrong during the installation process. Additionally, you should close all unnecessary applications and processes running on your computer. Installing VirtualBox is a resource-intensive task, and having too many applications open may lead to performance issues or conflicts during installation. Closing unnecessary programs helps free up system resources and minimizes the chance of interruptions. Another critical step in preparing your system is to disable or temporarily uninstall any antivirus or security software. While these applications are essential for protecting your computer, they may interfere with the VirtualBox installation process. Disabling or temporarily removing security software helps prevent conflicts and ensures a smooth installation. It's important to remember to re-enable or reinstall your security software once VirtualBox is successfully installed. Additionally, ensure that your computer is connected to a stable and high-speed internet connection. VirtualBox may need to download additional components or updates during installation. A reliable internet connection helps expedite this process and prevents potential interruptions. To avoid any unexpected issues, it's a good practice to disconnect any unnecessary external devices or peripherals from your computer before starting the installation. These devices may include external hard drives, USB devices, printers, or additional monitors. Disconnecting them reduces the chances of conflicts or driver-related problems during the installation. Before you begin the installation process, it's essential to obtain the latest version of the VirtualBox installer from the official VirtualBox website. Downloading the installer directly from the official source ensures that you are getting a legitimate and unaltered copy of the software. Avoid downloading VirtualBox from third-party websites to mitigate the risk of downloading potentially compromised or outdated versions. Once you have downloaded the VirtualBox installer, you should double-check its integrity by verifying the file's checksum. Checksum verification helps confirm that the downloaded file has not been tampered with or corrupted during the download process. Instructions for verifying the checksum can usually be found on the VirtualBox website alongside the download link. After confirming the integrity of the installer, you can proceed with the installation process. It's essential to run the installer with administrative privileges to ensure that it can make the necessary system changes. Right-click on the installer executable and select "Run as administrator" to initiate the installation. Throughout the installation process, you may encounter various prompts and options. It's important to read and follow the on-screen instructions carefully. These prompts may include options for customizing the installation, such as choosing specific components or installation directories. Customizing the installation allows you to tailor VirtualBox to your needs and preferences. During the installation, you may be prompted to install additional components or drivers, such as VirtualBox Guest Additions. These components enhance the functionality and integration between your host and guest operating systems within VirtualBox. It's generally advisable to install these additional components unless you have a specific reason not to. After the installation is complete, it's a good practice to restart your computer to ensure that any changes made during the installation process take effect. Restarting your computer helps finalize the

VirtualBox installation and ensures that the software operates smoothly. Once your computer has restarted, you can launch VirtualBox to start using the virtualization platform. Before creating virtual machines or importing virtual appliances, it's important to review and configure VirtualBox's settings to match your specific requirements. These settings may include preferences for virtual machine storage locations, network configurations, and advanced options. Customizing these settings allows you to optimize VirtualBox for your intended use. Finally, it's advisable to periodically check for updates to VirtualBox after installation. VirtualBox receives regular updates, which may include bug fixes, performance improvements, and new features. Keeping your VirtualBox installation up to date helps ensure that you have the latest enhancements and security patches. You can check for updates from within the VirtualBox application or by visiting the official VirtualBox website. In summary, preparing your system for VirtualBox installation involves several crucial steps to ensure a smooth and successful installation process. By checking system requirements, updating your host operating system, creating backups, closing unnecessary applications, disabling security software temporarily, and verifying the integrity of the installer, you can minimize the risk of installation issues. Once VirtualBox is installed, reviewing and configuring its settings to match your requirements and keeping the software up to date are essential practices for maximizing the benefits of virtualization on your computer.

Installing and configuring Guest Additions is a crucial step in getting the most out of your VirtualBox virtual machines. Guest Additions are a set of drivers and utilities that enhance the interaction between the host and guest operating systems within a virtual machine. These additions improve the performance, integration, and functionality of the guest operating system, making it feel more like a native system. To install Guest Additions, you should first ensure that your virtual machine is running and has been started from the VirtualBox Manager. Once your virtual machine is up and running, go to the "Devices" menu at the top of the virtual machine window and select "Insert Guest Additions CD image." This action will virtually insert the Guest Additions CD image into your virtual machine's optical drive. In most cases, the Guest Additions CD image will automatically run when you insert it into the virtual machine. However, if it doesn't, you can manually initiate the installation process by navigating to the optical drive within the guest operating system and running the installer. The installation process may require administrative or root privileges within the guest operating system. Follow the on-screen instructions provided by the Guest Additions installer to complete the installation. The installer will copy the necessary files and drivers to the guest operating system and make the required configurations. Once the installation is complete, you will need to restart your virtual machine to apply the changes made by Guest Additions. After restarting your virtual machine, you will begin to experience the benefits of Guest Additions.

One of the most significant advantages is improved display resolution. Guest Additions enable your virtual machine to dynamically adjust its screen resolution to match the size of the VirtualBox window. This feature makes it more convenient to work with your virtual machine, as it eliminates the need for manual resolution adjustments. Guest Additions also enhance mouse integration, allowing the mouse to seamlessly move between the host and guest operating systems. This integration makes it feel as if you are working on a native system, without the need to capture or release the mouse cursor explicitly. Furthermore, Guest Additions provide shared clipboard functionality. This feature enables you to copy and paste text and files between the host and guest operating systems, simplifying data transfer and enhancing productivity. To use the shared clipboard, simply copy text or files in one environment, and then paste them into the other. Guest Additions also offer the ability to share folders between the host and guest operating systems. This feature allows you to define specific folders on your host system that are accessible from within the virtual machine. Shared folders provide a convenient way to exchange data between the two environments. Configuring shared folders is typically done through the VirtualBox Manager, where you can specify which folders on the host system should be shared with the virtual machine. You can also define the folder's name and the type of access it grants to the guest operating system. For example, you can configure a shared folder as read-only or read-write, depending on your needs.

Once shared folders are configured, you can access them from within the guest operating system as network-mounted drives or directories, depending on the guest's operating system. This allows for seamless file exchange and data sharing between the host and guest environments. Another advantage of Guest Additions is the ability to enable and use 3D acceleration within the virtual machine. 3D acceleration improves the performance of graphics-intensive applications and allows for a more responsive user experience. Applications that rely on 3D graphics, such as games or 3D modeling software, benefit significantly from this feature. To enable 3D acceleration, you should go to the virtual machine's settings in the VirtualBox Manager and navigate to the "Display" section. There, you can check the box to enable 3D acceleration and specify the amount of video memory allocated to the virtual machine. Keep in mind that not all guest operating systems and virtual hardware configurations support 3D acceleration. You may need to install additional graphics drivers within the guest operating system to fully utilize this feature. Guest Additions also improve the performance of the virtual machine's audio subsystem. Enabling audio support through Guest Additions allows you to play sound within the virtual machine and use audio input devices, such as microphones, seamlessly. This feature is particularly valuable when using applications that rely on sound or voice communication. To configure audio support, you can go to the virtual machine's settings in the VirtualBox Manager and navigate to the "Audio" section. There, you can select the audio controller and audio output and input devices. Guest Additions provide an enhanced experience when working with the virtual machine's shared clipboard, shared folders, 3D acceleration, and audio subsystem. However, it's important to keep Guest Additions up to date to ensure compatibility with your VirtualBox version and guest operating system. As VirtualBox receives updates and improvements, new versions of Guest Additions may be released to provide better integration and functionality. To check for Guest Additions updates, you can visit the VirtualBox website or use the VirtualBox Manager's "Check for Updates" feature. Once you have updated Guest Additions, you can reinstall them in your virtual machines to benefit from the latest enhancements. In summary, installing and configuring Guest Additions is a crucial step in optimizing the performance and functionality of your virtual machines in VirtualBox. These additions enhance display resolution, mouse integration, shared clipboard functionality, and the ability to share folders between the host and guest operating systems. Additionally, they enable 3D acceleration and improve the virtual machine's audio subsystem. By following the installation and configuration steps, you can make your virtual machine experience more seamless and productive. Regularly checking for updates to Guest Additions ensures that you have access to the latest improvements and compatibility updates, enhancing your virtualization experience even further.

Chapter 3: Creating Your First Virtual Machine

Creating virtual machines is at the core of virtualization technology and is fundamental to harnessing its benefits. Before diving into the specifics of virtual machine creation, it's essential to understand the concept of a virtual machine (VM). A virtual machine is a software-based emulation of a physical computer that runs its own isolated operating system. This emulation allows multiple virtual machines to coexist on a single physical host, effectively partitioning the host's resources and enabling various operating systems to run concurrently. Virtual machines are self-contained entities with their own virtual CPUs, memory, storage, and network interfaces. To create a virtual machine, you'll typically start by launching a virtualization platform like VirtualBox. Once the virtualization software is running, you can begin the process of creating a new virtual machine. The first step in creating a virtual machine is to specify its basic characteristics. This includes choosing the type and version of the guest operating system that will run inside the virtual machine. Selecting the correct guest operating system type and version ensures that the virtualization software can provide optimal compatibility and settings for the VM. Next, you'll need to allocate system resources to the virtual machine. This involves specifying the amount of CPU cores, memory (RAM), and disk storage that the virtual machine will use. The allocation of resources depends on the requirements of the guest operating system and the workload you intend to run within the VM. Balancing resource allocation is essential to prevent overcommitting resources, which could lead to performance issues. Once you've defined the basic characteristics and allocated resources, you'll need to configure the virtual machine's storage settings. This includes creating a virtual hard disk or using an existing one to store the guest operating system and data. You can choose between dynamically allocated or fixed-size virtual hard disks, each with its own advantages and trade-offs. Dynamically allocated disks start small and grow as needed, while fixed-size disks allocate the entire space upfront. After setting up storage, you can configure the virtual machine's network settings. You can choose from various network modes, such as NAT, bridged, or host-only networking, depending on your networking requirements. These settings determine how the virtual machine communicates with the host and other devices on the network. Additionally, you can configure port forwarding and other network-related options to suit your specific needs. Once the virtual machine's basic settings are in place, you'll need to install the guest operating system. This involves selecting the installation media, which can be an ISO file, a physical CD/DVD, or a network installation source. You'll also need to specify the order in which the virtual machine should boot from these sources. After configuring the boot order and attaching the installation media, you can start the virtual machine. As the virtual machine boots up, it will load the guest operating system installation process. You'll follow the installation steps provided by the guest operating system, such as selecting language, timezone, and partitioning options. Throughout the installation process, the virtual machine will interact with the virtual hardware provided by the virtualization software. This interaction allows the guest operating system to detect and utilize the allocated CPU cores, memory, and storage resources. After completing the installation and configuring the guest operating system settings, you'll need to install virtualization-specific drivers and tools known as Guest Additions or Integration Services. These additions enhance the virtual machine's performance, integration, and functionality. They enable features such as dynamic screen resolution adjustment, seamless mouse integration, shared clipboard, and more. Installing these tools is essential for optimizing the virtual machine's usability. With the guest operating system installed and configured, the virtual machine is ready for use. You can run applications, host web servers, set up development environments, or perform any tasks that the guest operating system supports. Virtual machines provide a versatile and isolated environment for various use cases, such as software development, testing, server hosting, and more. Managing virtual machines is an ongoing process that includes tasks like creating snapshots, cloning, and adjusting resource allocations as needed. Snapshots capture the current state of the virtual machine, including its memory and storage contents. Creating snapshots allows you to save a point-in-time state of the virtual machine and revert to it if necessary. This feature is invaluable for testing and experimentation, as it provides a safety net for making changes to the virtual machine. Cloning allows you to duplicate virtual machines quickly. This is useful for deploying multiple identical virtual machines with the same configuration, reducing setup time and ensuring consistency. Resource management involves monitoring the performance and resource utilization of virtual machines. You can adjust CPU, memory, and storage allocations as workload requirements change, ensuring optimal performance and resource utilization. Many virtualization platforms also provide features for live migration, high availability, and load balancing to enhance the reliability and performance of virtual machines in enterprise environments. Virtual machines have become an integral part of modern computing environments, offering flexibility, scalability, and resource isolation. They enable efficient utilization of hardware resources and provide a platform for running diverse operating systems and workloads on a single physical host. Virtualization has revolutionized the way organizations deploy and manage IT infrastructure, allowing for increased agility and cost savings. As technology continues to evolve, virtualization will remain a crucial component of data centers, cloud computing, and software development environments. In summary, virtual machine creation is a foundational concept in virtualization technology, allowing multiple operating systems to coexist on a single physical host. Creating a virtual machine involves specifying basic characteristics, allocating resources, configuring storage and networking settings, and installing the guest operating system. Virtual machines offer a versatile and isolated environment for various tasks, with the ability to run applications, host servers, and perform testing and development. Managing virtual machines includes tasks such as creating snapshots, cloning, and resource management to ensure optimal performance and resource utilization. Virtualization has transformed IT infrastructure and will continue to play a pivotal role in the future of computing.

Setting up a virtual machine (VM) in VirtualBox is a step-by-step process that enables you to create a virtualized environment for running guest operating systems. Before you begin, make sure you have VirtualBox installed on your host system, as it is the platform that allows you to create and manage virtual machines. Once VirtualBox is installed, open the application to start the VM setup process. The first step in setting up a VM is to click the "New" button in the VirtualBox Manager interface. This action initiates the VM creation wizard, which guides you through the necessary configuration steps. In the wizard's first screen, you are prompted to enter a name for your virtual machine. Choose a descriptive name that reflects the purpose or type of guest operating system you plan to install. After naming your VM, you need to specify the type and version of the guest operating system. VirtualBox provides a list of preconfigured options for various operating systems, including different versions of Windows, Linux distributions, macOS, and more. Select the appropriate type and version that matches the guest operating system you intend to install. Once you've chosen the guest operating system type and version, the next step is to allocate memory (RAM) to your virtual machine. This step is essential because it determines how much system memory will be available to the guest operating system. Allocate an amount of memory that meets the requirements of your guest OS and the workloads you plan to run within the VM. Keep in mind that allocating too much memory to the VM may impact the performance of your host system, so strike a balance based on your available resources. The subsequent screen in the VM setup wizard prompts you to create a virtual hard disk for your virtual machine. A virtual hard disk is a file that acts as the storage device for the guest operating system and its data. You can either create a new virtual hard disk or use an existing one if you have one available. When creating a new virtual hard disk, you have the option to choose between a dynamically allocated disk and a fixed-size disk. A dynamically allocated disk starts with a small size and grows as the guest operating system and applications consume space. On the other hand, a fixed-size disk allocates all the specified disk space upfront. Choosing the type of virtual hard disk depends on your preferences and available storage. After defining your virtual hard disk, you need to specify its size. This is an important decision, as it determines how much storage capacity your virtual machine will have. Ensure that the virtual hard disk size is sufficient to accommodate the guest operating system, applications, and any additional data or files you plan to store within the VM. Consider the requirements of your specific use case when determining the disk size. Once you've configured the virtual hard disk, you'll be presented with an overview of your virtual machine's settings. Review the settings to ensure they align with your requirements, including the guest operating system type, memory allocation, and virtual hard disk details. If everything looks correct, click the "Create" button to proceed with the VM creation process. VirtualBox will then create the virtual machine and its associated settings based on your selections. With the virtual machine created, you can further fine-tune its settings to match your specific needs. Select the virtual machine from the VirtualBox Manager interface and click the "Settings" button. This will open the VM's settings, where you can configure various aspects of the virtual machine. Within the settings, you can adjust CPU allocation, enabling you to specify the number of virtual CPU cores assigned to the virtual machine. This setting allows you to allocate CPU resources based on the requirements of your guest operating system and applications. Additionally, you can configure the boot order of the virtual machine to determine which devices it should boot from. This is useful when you need to boot from a specific installation media, such as an ISO file or a CD/DVD drive. The "Display" settings allow you to customize the video memory, screen resolution, and enable 3D acceleration for improved graphics performance. These settings are essential for ensuring the virtual machine's display matches your preferences and requirements. The "Storage" settings allow you to manage the virtual machine's storage devices, including the virtual hard disk and any optical drives. You can attach or remove storage devices, change their order, and specify bootable devices. This flexibility allows you to configure the virtual machine's storage to meet your installation and data storage needs. Networking settings enable you to configure how the virtual machine connects to the network. VirtualBox provides various network modes, such as NAT, bridged, and host-only networking. Select the networking mode that aligns with your network requirements and connectivity preferences. Advanced settings, such as port forwarding, allow you to customize network configurations further. Shared folders settings enable you to set up shared folders between your host system and the virtual machine. Shared folders simplify file sharing and data exchange between the two environments. You can specify which folders on your host system should be accessible from within the virtual machine and choose their access permissions. Finally, the "General" settings provide options for configuring the virtual machine's behavior, including enabling or disabling features like clipboard sharing and drag-and-drop support. These settings can enhance your overall virtual machine experience by enabling seamless interaction between the host and guest systems. After configuring the virtual machine's settings to your satisfaction, you can proceed to install the guest operating system. To do this, select the virtual machine from the VirtualBox Manager interface and click the "Start" button. This action launches the virtual machine, and it will boot from the selected installation media, such as an ISO file or a physical CD/DVD. Follow the installation instructions provided by the guest operating system to complete the installation. Once the guest operating system is installed, you can install additional software and configure the virtual machine as needed for your specific use case. Remember that managing and maintaining your virtual machine is an ongoing process. You can create snapshots of the virtual machine's state to capture specific configurations or system states. Snapshots provide a safety net, allowing you to revert to a previous state if issues arise or changes need to be rolled back. Regularly updating the guest operating system and any installed software within the virtual machine is essential to ensure security and compatibility. Additionally, monitoring resource usage and adjusting resource allocations as necessary helps maintain optimal virtual machine performance. In summary, setting up a virtual machine in VirtualBox is a systematic process that involves creating a virtual machine, configuring its settings, and installing a guest operating system. Carefully consider the guest operating system type, resource allocation, and storage configuration to create a virtual machine tailored to your needs. Fine-tuning settings, such as CPU allocation, display options, and networking, allows you to customize the virtual machine further. After installation, managing and maintaining the virtual machine includes creating snapshots, updating software, and monitoring resource usage to ensure optimal performance and functionality.

Chapter 4: Configuring Virtual Networks in VirtualBox

Virtual networking in VirtualBox is a critical aspect of creating and managing virtual machines, as it enables communication and connectivity between virtual machines, the host system, and external networks. Understanding virtual networking is essential for configuring and optimizing your virtualized environment. At its core, virtual networking in VirtualBox simulates the functionality of physical network hardware within a virtualized environment. This simulation allows virtual machines to communicate with each other and with external networks, just as physical computers do. VirtualBox provides several networking modes and configurations to meet various use cases and requirements. The default networking mode in VirtualBox is known as NAT, which stands for Network Address Translation. In NAT mode, the virtual machine shares the host system's network connection through a virtual NAT router. This configuration allows the virtual machine to access external networks and the internet, but it also isolates it from direct inbound network connections. The NAT router acts as an intermediary, translating network traffic between the virtual machine and the external network. While NAT mode provides internet connectivity for virtual machines, it does not allow external systems to initiate connections to the virtual machines. If you need to expose services running within a virtual machine to external systems, you can use port forwarding. Port forwarding allows you to map specific ports on the host system to ports on the virtual machine, enabling external access to services hosted within the VM. Another networking mode available in VirtualBox is Bridged Networking. In Bridged mode, the virtual machine becomes a full-fledged member of the host's network, just like any other physical device. It obtains an IP address from the same DHCP server used by the host system, allowing it to communicate directly with other devices on the network. Bridged Networking is suitable for scenarios where you need the virtual machine to have its own IP address on the local network, such as when hosting web servers or other network services. Host-Only Networking is another virtual networking mode provided by VirtualBox. In this mode, the virtual machine can communicate with the host system and other virtual machines connected to the same Host-Only network, but it cannot access external networks or the internet. Host-Only Networking is useful for creating isolated environments where virtual machines can communicate with each other and the host system, making it ideal for development and testing purposes. You can create multiple Host-Only networks in VirtualBox, each functioning as a separate isolated network segment. Internal Networking is a networking mode that allows virtual machines to communicate with each other but not with the host system or external networks. This mode is suitable for creating isolated network environments solely for the interaction between virtual machines. Internal Networking is often used for testing network configurations, simulating multi-tier application architectures, or experimenting with network services. Virtual networking in VirtualBox also includes a feature called Generic Networking, which allows you to use custom network stack implementations or third-party tools to define the networking behavior of a virtual machine. This advanced feature is typically used in specialized scenarios where standard networking modes do not provide the required functionality. To configure virtual networking for a virtual machine, you can access the network settings for that specific VM. Select the virtual machine in the VirtualBox Manager interface, click the "Settings" button, and navigate to the "Network" section. Here, you can choose the desired networking mode, configure additional options, and set up port forwarding if necessary. For Bridged Networking and Host-Only Networking, you can also select the network interface on the host system to which the virtual machine should be attached. Advanced users may explore additional network settings, such as MAC address assignment and adapter type. Once you have configured the virtual machine's network settings, you can start the VM to apply the changes. The virtual machine will then use the specified networking mode and settings for its network connectivity. Managing virtual networking also includes monitoring network traffic, ensuring proper routing and connectivity, and troubleshooting any network-related issues. You can use standard networking tools and utilities within the guest operating system to diagnose and resolve network problems. Additionally, VirtualBox provides logging and diagnostic features to help identify and address networking issues within the virtualization platform. It's essential to keep your virtual machine's network configurations in line with your specific requirements and security considerations. For example, when setting up port forwarding, ensure that only the necessary ports are exposed to external systems, and regularly review and update these configurations as needed. When using Bridged Networking, pay attention to the IP address assignments to prevent IP conflicts on the local network. Furthermore, Host-Only Networking should be used judiciously to maintain the isolation and security of virtual machines. In summary, virtual networking in VirtualBox is a crucial component of creating and managing virtual machines. Understanding the various networking modes, such as NAT, Bridged Networking, Host-Only Networking, and Internal Networking, allows you to configure virtualized environments to suit your specific use cases and requirements. Properly configuring and managing virtual networking ensures that virtual machines can communicate with each other, the host system, and external networks as needed. Regular monitoring, troubleshooting, and security considerations are essential aspects of effectively managing virtual networking in VirtualBox. Setting up and managing virtual networks is a crucial aspect of modern computing environments, enabling organizations and individuals to create isolated and interconnected network environments within a virtualized infrastructure. Virtual networks provide flexibility, scalability, and security, allowing multiple virtual machines to communicate while maintaining separation from the physical network. Whether you are a system administrator responsible for an enterprise network or an individual setting up virtualized labs for testing and development, understanding how to create and manage virtual networks is essential. Virtual networks are software-defined network segments that operate independently of physical network hardware. They are often used in conjunction with virtualization platforms like VirtualBox, VMware, and Hyper-V to connect virtual machines to each other, to the host system, and to external networks. One of the fundamental virtual network concepts is network isolation, which ensures that virtual machines within one virtual network cannot directly communicate with those in another. This isolation is crucial for maintaining security and separation between different environments, such as development, testing, and production. To set up and manage virtual networks effectively, you need to choose an appropriate virtualization platform and understand its networking capabilities. Each virtualization platform provides different networking modes and features, and the specific options may vary. For example, VirtualBox offers NAT, Bridged Networking, Host-Only Networking, and Internal Networking, while VMware provides similar but differently named networking modes. Selecting the right networking mode depends on your specific use case and requirements. NAT (Network Address

Translation) mode is commonly used to provide internet access to virtual machines while maintaining isolation from external networks. In NAT mode, the virtualization platform acts as a network router, allowing virtual machines to share the host system's network connection. Bridged Networking, on the other hand, integrates virtual machines into the physical network by providing them with unique IP addresses on the same network segment as the host system. This mode is suitable for scenarios where virtual machines need full network access and communication with external devices. Host-Only Networking creates a separate network segment that includes the host system and all virtual machines configured for Host-Only mode. This mode is ideal for creating isolated network environments for development, testing, or simulating network configurations. Internal Networking enables communication between virtual machines on a shared internal network but isolates them from external networks. Selecting the appropriate networking mode depends on factors like network connectivity requirements, security concerns, and the need for isolation. Once you've chosen a networking mode, you need to configure it according to your requirements. This includes setting IP addresses, subnet masks, and gateway addresses to define the network's structure. Virtual networks often use private IP address ranges, such as those defined by RFC 1918, to avoid IP conflicts with external networks. For example, the 192.168.0.0/16 or 10.0.0.0/8 address ranges are commonly used for virtual networks. When configuring virtual networks, it's essential to ensure that IP address assignments do not conflict with the physical network's IP address space. You should also consider setting up DNS and DHCP servers within the virtual network to manage IP address assignments and provide name resolution services. Managing virtual networks involves ongoing tasks to monitor and maintain network performance, security, and connectivity. Regularly monitoring network traffic and resource utilization can help identify bottlenecks and address performance issues promptly. Security considerations are critical, as virtual networks may contain sensitive data or systems. Implementing firewalls, access controls, and encryption can help safeguard virtual network resources. Regularly updating virtualization platform and virtual machine software is essential to patch vulnerabilities and ensure security. In addition to security, optimizing network performance is crucial to ensure efficient communication between virtual machines. This includes configuring Quality of Service (QoS) settings, load balancing, and optimizing network traffic routing. Virtualization platforms often provide tools and utilities for managing virtual networks, such as network configuration wizards and monitoring dashboards. These tools simplify the process of creating, configuring, and maintaining virtual networks. When creating virtual networks, you may also need to consider more advanced network features like VLANs (Virtual LANs) and VPNs (Virtual Private Networks). VLANs allow you to segment a physical network into multiple isolated logical networks, each with its own set of virtual machines. This segmentation enhances network security and reduces broadcast traffic. VPNs enable secure communication between virtual machines located in different virtual networks or even across physical networks. Implementing a VPN can ensure encrypted and private communication between virtual machines, adding an extra layer of security to your virtualized environment. Furthermore, virtualization platforms often support the creation of complex network topologies, such as multi-tier application architectures. These topologies can include web servers, application servers, and database servers connected in a specific arrangement to mimic real-world scenarios. Creating such topologies allows for testing, development, and troubleshooting of complex network configurations. Overall, setting up and managing virtual networks is a critical skill for system administrators, IT professionals, and developers working with virtualized environments. Understanding the available networking modes, configuring IP addresses and network services, and implementing security measures are essential steps in creating and maintaining effective virtual networks. By mastering virtual networking concepts and best practices, you can harness the full potential of virtualization technology, whether for personal projects, testing, development, or enterprise-level deployments.

Chapter 5: Managing Virtual Storage in VirtualBox

Storage management is a fundamental aspect of virtualization, and in VirtualBox, it plays a crucial role in creating, configuring, and managing virtual machines. Understanding storage management basics is essential for optimizing performance, ensuring data integrity, and efficiently utilizing storage resources within your virtualized environment. In VirtualBox, each virtual machine (VM) requires storage to host the guest operating system, applications, and data. This storage is typically represented as one or more virtual hard disks, which are files on the host system's physical storage. Virtual hard disks can be thought of as the equivalent of physical hard drives in a traditional computer. When creating a virtual machine in VirtualBox, one of the primary storage-related decisions is to determine the size and type of virtual hard disk(s) that the VM will use. Virtual hard disks come in two main types: dynamically allocated and fixed size. Dynamically allocated disks start small and grow in size as the guest operating system and applications consume storage space. This type of disk is advantageous because it optimizes physical storage usage by allocating space only when needed. However, it may have slightly slower performance as the disk grows. On the other hand, fixed-size disks allocate the entire specified storage space upfront when they are created. These disks provide consistent and often better performance but use more physical storage from the start. Choosing between these two types depends on your specific requirements, including performance and storage utilization considerations. Once you've decided on the type of virtual hard disk, you'll need to specify the size. The size of the virtual hard disk should be sufficient to accommodate the guest operating system, applications, and data that will be stored within the virtual machine. Consider the requirements of your specific use case when determining the disk size. It's important to note that you can create multiple virtual hard disks for a single virtual machine, each serving different purposes. For example, you may have a smaller virtual hard disk for the guest operating system and a separate, larger virtual hard disk for data storage. This separation allows you to manage and back up data independently from the operating system. VirtualBox also provides the option to use existing virtual hard disks or to create new ones when setting up a virtual machine. Using existing virtual hard disks can be beneficial when you have preconfigured disk images that you want to reuse for multiple virtual machines. Once you have created or selected the virtual hard disks for your virtual machine, it's time to attach them. Attaching a virtual hard disk to a virtual machine is similar to connecting a physical hard drive to a physical computer. You specify the virtual hard disk(s) that the virtual machine should use when configuring the VM's storage settings. VirtualBox allows you to add or remove virtual hard disks from a virtual machine at any time, providing flexibility in managing storage. After attaching the virtual hard disks, you'll need to decide on the order in which the virtual machine should boot from these disks. This boot order determines which virtual hard disk is used as the primary boot device and which is used as secondary storage. It's an essential consideration when you need to install a guest operating system or manage multiple virtual hard disks with different purposes. Virtual hard disks in VirtualBox are typically stored as files on the host system's physical storage. These files can be located in a directory of your choosing, and VirtualBox offers the option to specify the location when creating the virtual hard disk. It's advisable to organize these files in a structured manner to keep your virtual machine configurations tidy and easily accessible. In addition to virtual hard disks, VirtualBox also supports other types of storage, such as optical drives (CD/DVD) and floppy drives. You can attach ISO image files or physical CD/DVD drives to virtual machines to boot from installation media or access data. This feature is useful when installing or repairing guest operating systems or using software that requires physical media. Once the virtual machine is configured with the appropriate storage resources, you can start the VM and proceed with the guest operating system installation. During the installation process, the virtual machine will interact with the virtual hard disks, reading and writing data as needed. It's essential to monitor the storage usage of your virtual machines regularly to prevent running out of space. Running out of storage can lead to issues, including data corruption and performance degradation. VirtualBox provides tools and utilities for managing and monitoring storage resources within virtual machines. Additionally, it's crucial to back up the virtual hard disks and regularly back up the data stored within virtual machines to prevent data loss in the event of hardware failure or other unforeseen circumstances. Snapshotting is another storage management feature offered by VirtualBox. Snapshots capture the current state of a virtual machine, including its memory and storage contents. Creating snapshots allows you to save a point-in-time state of the virtual machine and revert to it if necessary. This feature is invaluable for testing and experimentation, as it provides a safety net for making changes to the virtual machine. Managing storage in VirtualBox also involves considering performance optimization. Optimizing storage performance ensures that virtual machines operate efficiently and that data access is smooth. One way to improve storage performance is by using SSDs (Solid-State Drives) for hosting virtual hard disks, as they offer faster read and write speeds compared to traditional HDDs (Hard Disk Drives). Another technique is to use the VirtualBox Guest Additions or VMware Tools, depending on your virtualization platform, within the guest operating system. These tools provide enhanced storage drivers and features that improve storage performance, such as TRIM support for SSDs and optimized storage controllers. To conclude, understanding storage management basics in VirtualBox is essential for creating and managing virtual machines efficiently. Key considerations include choosing the type and size of virtual hard disks, configuring boot orders, and attaching storage devices like optical drives. Regular monitoring, backup strategies, and the use of features like snapshots contribute to effective storage management. By mastering these fundamentals, you can ensure the smooth operation and data integrity of your virtualized environment.

Configuring and managing virtual disks is a fundamental aspect of virtualization, allowing you to allocate storage resources to virtual machines efficiently. Virtual disks serve as the equivalent of physical hard drives in a virtualized environment, and understanding how to configure and manage them is essential for optimizing performance and ensuring data integrity. In virtualization platforms like VMware, VirtualBox, and Hyper-V, virtual disks are created to store the guest operating system, applications, and data for virtual machines. These virtual disks are stored as files on the host system's physical storage. When configuring virtual disks, one of the first decisions is to choose the type of virtual disk. The type of virtual disk determines how the virtual machine interacts with the storage medium and affects factors like performance and flexibility. The most common types of virtual disks include fixed-size, dynamically allocated, and differencing disks. A fixed-size virtual disk allocates all the specified storage space upfront, guaranteeing consistent performance but consuming more physical storage space. Dynamically allocated virtual disks start small and grow as the guest operating system and applications consume storage space, optimizing physical storage usage but potentially leading to some performance variability. Differencing disks, also known as snapshots or delta disks, are used to capture changes made to a base virtual disk over time, allowing you to revert to previous states. Once you've chosen the type of virtual disk, the next step is to determine the size. The size of the virtual disk should be sufficient to accommodate the guest operating system, applications, and data that will be stored within the virtual machine. It's crucial to consider the storage requirements of your specific use case to avoid running out of space. Virtualization platforms typically provide options for creating virtual disks during the virtual machine setup process. For example, in VMware, you can select the disk type and specify the size when configuring the virtual machine's hardware settings. After creating a virtual disk, you can attach it to the virtual machine, effectively providing storage for the guest operating system and applications. Virtual disks can be added or removed from a virtual machine as needed, providing flexibility in managing storage resources. When attaching virtual disks, you can specify the boot order to determine which disk the virtual machine should use as the primary boot device. This is essential when you need to install a guest operating system or manage multiple virtual disks with different purposes. It's worth noting that virtual disks are typically stored as files on the host system's physical storage. These files can be organized within a directory structure of your choice, making it easier to manage virtual machine configurations and their associated virtual disks. Regularly monitoring storage usage is crucial to prevent running out of space, which can lead to performance issues and data corruption. To monitor storage usage, you can use the tools and utilities provided by the virtualization platform, such as storage management dashboards and reports. It's also essential to implement a backup strategy for virtual disks and the data stored within virtual machines. Regularly backing up virtual disks and data helps prevent data loss in case of hardware failures or other unforeseen circumstances. In addition to backups, snapshotting is a valuable feature offered by virtualization platforms. Snapshots capture the current state of a virtual machine, including its storage contents, and allow you to revert to that state if needed. This feature is particularly useful for testing, experimentation, and creating restore points before making significant changes to a virtual machine. Performance optimization is another consideration when configuring and managing virtual disks. Optimizing storage performance ensures that virtual machines operate efficiently, and data access is smooth. One way to improve storage performance is by using SSDs (Solid-State Drives) for hosting virtual disks, as they offer faster read and write speeds compared to traditional HDDs (Hard Disk Drives). Another technique is to use storage optimization features provided by the virtualization platform, such as thin provisioning and storage caching. Thin provisioning allows you to allocate storage on-demand, reducing initial storage consumption and optimizing resource utilization. Storage caching can improve read and write performance by using high-speed storage devices or caching algorithms to accelerate data access. To optimize performance further, consider using virtualization platform-specific tools like VMware Tools or VirtualBox Guest Additions. These tools provide enhanced storage drivers and features that can improve storage performance, such as TRIM support for SSDs and optimized storage controllers. Managing virtual disks also involves considering security measures to protect data stored within virtual machines. Implementing encryption for virtual disks can safeguard data from unauthorized access, even if the virtual disk files are accessed directly. In some cases, encryption can be managed by the virtualization platform itself or through external encryption solutions. It's essential to stay up-to-date with security best practices and regularly apply patches and updates to both the virtualization platform and the guest operating systems within virtual machines. To summarize, configuring and managing virtual disks is a vital aspect of virtualization that directly impacts the performance, reliability, and security of virtualized environments. Key considerations include choosing the type and size of virtual disks, configuring boot orders, and attaching storage devices. Regular monitoring, backup strategies, and the use of features like snapshots contribute to effective storage management. Performance optimization and security measures help ensure efficient operation and data protection within virtualized environments. By mastering these fundamentals, you can maximize the benefits of virtualization technology for both personal and enterprise-level deployments.

Chapter 6: Snapshots and Cloning in VirtualBox

Understanding snapshots in VirtualBox is essential for effectively managing the state of virtual machines and ensuring system stability in virtualized environments. Snapshots are a powerful feature that allows you to capture the current state of a virtual machine, including its memory and storage contents, and save it as a reference point. Snapshots are particularly valuable for tasks like system backup, testing, and experimentation, as they provide a safety net for making changes to virtual machines without the risk of data loss or system corruption. To create a snapshot in VirtualBox, you start by selecting the virtual machine you want to snapshot and then navigating to the "Machine" menu in the VirtualBox Manager interface. From there, you can choose the "Take Snapshot" option and provide a name and description for the snapshot. This information helps you identify and manage snapshots later, especially when dealing with multiple snapshots of the same virtual machine. When you create a snapshot, VirtualBox captures the virtual machine's current state, which includes its memory contents, CPU state, and the contents of its virtual hard disks. The snapshot is stored as a separate file, separate from the original virtual machine's configuration and storage files. The process is relatively quick, and once the snapshot is created, you can continue using the virtual machine as usual. Snapshots create a point-in-time reference of the virtual machine, allowing you to revert to that specific state if needed. This can be extremely useful for various scenarios, such as testing software updates, installing new applications, or experimenting with system configurations. When you need to roll back to a snapshot, you simply select the snapshot you want to restore to and choose the "Restore" option from the VirtualBox Manager interface. VirtualBox will then return the virtual machine to the state it was in when the snapshot was taken. This includes restoring memory, CPU state, and the contents of virtual hard disks. It's important to note that when you restore a snapshot, any changes made to the virtual machine after that snapshot was taken will be lost. For example, if you create a snapshot of a virtual machine and then install software, the installation will be undone if you later restore to the snapshot. This is why it's essential to carefully manage snapshots and plan their use based on your specific needs. Snapshots in VirtualBox support a branching feature, allowing you to create multiple snapshots in a sequence. These snapshots create a tree-like structure, where each snapshot can have child snapshots. This branching feature is valuable for creating complex testing scenarios or managing multiple system states within the same virtual machine. For example, you could have a base snapshot representing a clean system installation and then create child snapshots for different software configurations or testing scenarios. Each child snapshot captures changes made to the parent snapshot, allowing you to maintain separate lines of development or experimentation.

While snapshots offer many advantages, they also come with some considerations and limitations. One limitation is that snapshots consume additional storage space on the host system's storage drive. Each snapshot file represents a point-in-time state of the virtual machine, and as you create more snapshots, storage usage increases. It's crucial to monitor storage usage regularly, especially if you plan to keep multiple snapshots for an extended period. Deleting snapshots is one way to free up storage space, and VirtualBox provides options to delete individual snapshots or entire snapshot trees. However, it's essential to understand that deleting a snapshot may affect the integrity of other snapshots in the same branch. For example, if you delete an intermediate snapshot in a branch, all child snapshots that rely on it will become invalid. Additionally, the process of deleting snapshots can take some time, especially if there are many snapshots or large virtual hard disks involved. Another consideration is performance. Snapshots can affect virtual machine performance, particularly as the snapshot tree grows. While creating a snapshot is a relatively quick process, the act of restoring to a snapshot or merging snapshots back into the base virtual machine can be resource-intensive. It's essential to plan your snapshot strategy with performance in mind, especially if you are working with virtual machines that have limited CPU and memory resources. When using snapshots, it's also vital to keep track of the snapshot hierarchy and the relationships between snapshots. Careful management helps prevent confusion and ensures that you can revert to the desired system state when needed. VirtualBox provides a snapshot manager that allows you to view and manage all the snapshots associated with a virtual machine. This manager displays the snapshot tree structure, making it easy to understand the relationships between snapshots. In addition to using snapshots for system backup, testing, and experimentation, they can also serve as a valuable tool for troubleshooting. If a problem arises within a virtual machine, and you suspect that recent changes may have caused it, you can revert to a snapshot taken before those changes were made. This can help isolate the issue and determine whether it is related to recent modifications or an underlying system problem. Overall, snapshots in VirtualBox are a versatile feature that can significantly enhance your virtualization experience. By understanding how to create, manage, and use snapshots effectively, you can make your virtual machines more flexible, reliable, and easier to maintain. Snapshots provide a valuable safety net for managing system changes and are a valuable asset for anyone working with virtualized environments, whether for personal projects or enterprise-level deployments.

Cloning and copying virtual machines are essential techniques in the realm of virtualization, offering the ability to duplicate existing virtual machines for various purposes. These processes provide efficiency, flexibility, and convenience in managing virtual environments. Cloning typically involves creating an identical replica of a virtual machine, including its configuration, installed software, and data. It's akin to producing a carbon copy of a physical computer, allowing you to create multiple instances of the same system configuration quickly. Copying, on the other hand, involves duplicating the virtual machine's files and configurations to create a separate, independent instance. While it may share some similarities with cloning, copying doesn't necessarily result in identical virtual machines. Both cloning and copying have their advantages and use cases, depending on the specific needs of your virtualization environment. Cloning is particularly useful when you require multiple virtual machines with identical configurations. For instance, in a development or testing environment, you may need several virtual machines with the same operating system, software versions, and settings. By cloning a virtual machine, you save time and ensure consistency across multiple instances. Virtualization platforms like VMware, VirtualBox, and Hyper-V offer built-in tools and features to facilitate cloning. These tools typically allow you to select a source virtual machine, specify a new name for the cloned machine, and configure networking options. Once the cloning process is complete, you have a new virtual machine that is an exact replica of the source, ready for use. Copying, on the other hand, provides more flexibility in terms of customization. When you copy a virtual machine, you create a duplicate of the virtual machine's files, including the virtual hard disks, configuration files, and snapshots. However, you can then make changes to the copied virtual machine, such as altering its configuration, installing additional software, or applying unique settings. This flexibility is valuable when you need similar but not identical virtual machines. For example, you might copy a base virtual machine with a specific operating system and then customize each copy for different purposes, such as web servers, application servers, or database servers. Copying is also useful when you want to move a virtual machine to a different host system or share it with others. You can copy the virtual machine's files to a new location or share them with colleagues, allowing them to run the virtual machine on their own systems. When copying a virtual machine, it's essential to consider the potential impact on networking settings. If the virtual machine you're copying uses static IP addresses or has network-specific configurations, you may need to adjust these settings to avoid conflicts. Additionally, some virtualization platforms offer features like "sysprep" or "guest customization" that allow you to prepare virtual machines for duplication. These features can automate the process of customizing virtual machines after they've been copied or cloned, ensuring that each instance has unique network settings, hostname, and other identifiers. Another important aspect to consider when cloning or copying virtual machines is the virtual hard disk. Virtual hard disks are typically included in the duplication process, and their size can significantly impact storage requirements. Therefore, it's crucial to monitor storage usage and plan for adequate disk space when working with cloned or copied virtual machines. Managing snapshots is another consideration when dealing with cloned or copied virtual machines. Snapshots capture the state of a virtual machine at a specific point in time, including its memory and storage contents. When you clone or copy a virtual machine, you may inherit its existing snapshots. This can be beneficial when you want to create new virtual machines with a specific system state. However, it's essential to understand the snapshot hierarchy and potential disk space implications. Snapshots consume storage space, and if not managed correctly, they can lead to storage issues. Before finalizing the cloning or copying process, it's advisable to review the snapshot configuration and decide whether to keep, merge, or discard existing snapshots. Ultimately, the choice between cloning and copying depends on your specific requirements and objectives. If you need identical virtual machines for consistent testing or development environments, cloning is the preferred method. On the other hand, if you require flexibility in customizing virtual machines for various purposes or need to move virtual machines to different host systems, copying provides the necessary versatility. Regardless of the method you choose, understanding the implications and best practices for cloning and copying virtual machines is essential for efficient virtualization management. By mastering these techniques, you can make the most of your virtualization platform and streamline your virtual machine deployment and management processes.

Chapter 7: Backup and Recovery Strategies

The importance of backups in virtual environments cannot be overstated, as they are a critical component of data protection and disaster recovery strategies. In today's digital age, data is the lifeblood of organizations, and ensuring its availability and integrity is paramount. Virtualization technology has revolutionized IT infrastructure by consolidating multiple virtual machines on a single physical server, enhancing resource utilization and scalability. However, this consolidation also means that a single point of failure could impact multiple virtual machines, making data backup and recovery essential. The benefits of virtualization, including flexibility and cost savings, can be jeopardized if adequate backup measures are not in place. Data loss or system failures in virtual environments can result from various factors, such as hardware failures, software errors, cyberattacks, or human errors. Without proper backups, these incidents can have catastrophic consequences, including prolonged downtime, financial losses, and reputational damage. Backing up virtual environments involves creating copies of virtual machines, their configurations, and data to an external storage medium or offsite location. These backups serve as insurance, allowing organizations to recover lost or corrupted data and quickly restore virtual machines to a working state. One of the key advantages of virtualization is its ability to create snapshots, which capture the state of a virtual machine at a specific moment. Snapshots can be used for data recovery and system rollback, providing a valuable layer of protection against unexpected issues. However, snapshots are not a complete substitute for regular backups because they are typically stored on the same infrastructure as the virtual machines themselves. In the event of hardware failures or other catastrophic events affecting the host server, both the virtual machines and their snapshots could be at risk. To address this vulnerability, organizations must implement comprehensive backup solutions designed explicitly for virtual environments. These solutions provide features such as image-based backups, deduplication, compression, and encryption, ensuring the secure and efficient storage of virtual machine data. Automated backup schedules can be established to create regular backups of virtual machines, reducing the risk of data loss and minimizing the impact of system failures. Backup strategies should be tailored to the specific needs and objectives of the organization, taking into account factors like recovery time objectives (RTOs) and recovery point objectives (RPOs). RTO defines the maximum acceptable downtime, while RPO determines the allowable data loss in case of a disaster. Virtualization allows for various backup approaches, including full backups, incremental backups, and differential backups. Full backups capture the entire virtual machine, while incremental backups record only the changes made since the last backup. Differential backups, on the other hand, save the differences between the current state and the last full backup. Each method has its advantages and trade-offs, and the choice depends on factors like storage capacity, backup speed, and recovery requirements. Backup solutions for virtual environments also support backup rotation and retention policies, allowing organizations to manage storage space efficiently. Older backups can be automatically purged or moved to long-term storage, ensuring that the backup repository remains manageable over time. Furthermore, backup solutions often provide versioning capabilities, allowing organizations to restore virtual machines to specific points in time. This feature is invaluable for recovering from data corruption or malware attacks that may not be immediately detected. In virtual environments, it's essential to consider the interplay between virtualization and backup technologies. Backup solutions designed for virtualization are aware of the virtual machine structure and can leverage features like VMware vSphere's vStorage APIs or Microsoft Hyper-V's VSS (Volume Shadow Copy Service) integration for efficient and consistent backups. These integration points enable the backup software to quiesce the virtual machine, ensuring that data is in a stable state before the backup process begins. As organizations embrace cloud computing and hybrid environments, backup solutions for virtual environments have adapted to offer cloud-based backup and disaster recovery options. Cloud backups provide offsite storage and recovery capabilities, reducing reliance on on-premises infrastructure and enhancing data availability. Backing up virtual machines to the cloud ensures that data remains accessible even if the primary data center experiences a major outage or disaster. Organizations can choose between public cloud providers like AWS, Azure, or Google Cloud, or opt for private cloud solutions to maintain full control over data and compliance. Additionally, cloud-based backups offer scalability and cost-effective storage options, aligning with the dynamic nature of virtualized environments. Effective backup strategies for virtual environments also consider data retention policies and compliance requirements. Depending on the industry and regulatory framework, organizations may be obligated to retain backups for a specific duration and ensure data integrity. Backup solutions often provide features like encryption and access controls to safeguard sensitive data and meet compliance standards. Regular testing of backup and recovery processes is a critical component of any backup strategy. Organizations should conduct periodic recovery drills to validate the effectiveness of their backup solutions and ensure that they can restore virtual machines and data in a timely manner. These tests help identify any gaps or issues in the backup and recovery processes, allowing for adjustments and improvements. Ultimately, the importance of backups in virtual environments extends beyond data protection and disaster recovery. Backups provide peace of mind, enabling organizations to embrace virtualization's benefits while mitigating the risks associated with system failures and data loss. In today's digital landscape, where data is a strategic asset, safeguarding its availability and integrity is a top priority. Backup solutions tailored for virtualization help organizations achieve this goal, ensuring business continuity and resilience in the face of unforeseen challenges. By embracing a comprehensive backup strategy, organizations can fully harness the potential of virtualization technology while safeguarding their most valuable asset: their data.

Backup and recovery best practices in VirtualBox are essential for safeguarding your virtual machines and data in a virtualized environment. Virtualization offers numerous advantages, but it also introduces new challenges when it comes to protecting and restoring virtual machines. By following these best practices, you can ensure the availability, integrity, and resilience of your virtualized infrastructure. One of the fundamental principles of backup and recovery is establishing a well-defined backup strategy. This strategy should consider factors such as recovery time objectives (RTOs), recovery point objectives (RPOs), and the criticality of virtual machines. RTO defines the maximum allowable downtime for a virtual machine, while RPO specifies the acceptable data loss in case of a failure. Understanding these objectives helps you tailor your backup strategy to meet specific business requirements. Regular backups are essential in a virtualized environment, as they enable you to restore virtual machines to a known good state in case of data loss or system failures. VirtualBox provides a snapshot feature that captures the current state of a virtual machine, including its memory and disk contents. Snapshots are a valuable tool for quick recovery and testing changes, but they should not be the sole backup method. Using dedicated backup solutions for VirtualBox ensures comprehensive protection and meets backup retention policies. Automated backup schedules can be established to create regular backups of virtual machines, minimizing the risk of data loss. Consider using full backups, incremental backups, or differential backups, depending on your storage capacity and recovery requirements. Full backups capture the entire virtual machine, while incremental backups record changes since the last backup. Differential backups save changes between the current state and the last full backup. Each method has its advantages and trade-offs, so choose the one that best aligns with your organization's needs. Storage capacity is a critical consideration in backup and recovery. As virtual machines grow in size and complexity, backups can consume significant storage space. Ensure that you have sufficient storage capacity for both backups and retained versions. Implementing a backup retention policy helps manage storage efficiently. Older backups can be automatically purged or moved to long-term storage, keeping the backup repository manageable. Versioning capabilities are essential for recovering from data corruption or malware attacks that may not be immediately detected. VirtualBox provides versioning through snapshot management and storage. You can roll back to a specific snapshot to restore a virtual machine to a known good state. When choosing a backup solution for VirtualBox, consider integration with snapshot management to streamline the process. Testing backup and recovery procedures is critical to ensure they work as expected. Regularly conduct recovery drills to validate the effectiveness of your backup strategy. These tests help identify any gaps or issues in the backup and recovery processes, allowing for adjustments and improvements. Ensure that backup and recovery documentation is comprehensive and accessible to the relevant personnel. Documentation should include step-by-step procedures for initiating backups, restoring virtual machines, and performing recovery tests. In a virtualized environment, it's essential to consider the interplay between virtualization and backup technologies. Backup solutions designed for VirtualBox are aware of the virtual machine structure and can leverage features like snapshot integration for efficient and consistent backups. These integration points enable the backup software to quiesce the virtual machine, ensuring that data is in a stable state before the backup process begins. Protecting backups is as crucial as backing up virtual machines themselves. Implement access controls and encryption to safeguard backup files and ensure that only authorized personnel can access them. Consider offsite or cloud-based backup solutions for added protection. Cloud backups provide offsite storage and recovery capabilities, reducing reliance on on-premises infrastructure and enhancing data availability. Backing up virtual machines to the cloud ensures that data remains accessible even if the primary data center experiences a major outage or disaster. Organizations can choose between public cloud providers like AWS, Azure, or Google Cloud, or opt for private cloud solutions to maintain full control over data and compliance. Backup solutions should provide features like image-based backups, deduplication, compression, and encryption to ensure the secure and efficient storage of virtual machine data. These features help optimize storage usage and protect sensitive information. Regularly update and patch both VirtualBox and the guest operating systems within virtual machines. Keeping software up-to-date helps prevent security vulnerabilities and ensures compatibility with backup solutions. Performing regular maintenance and monitoring of backup processes is essential to catch issues early. Automated alerts and notifications can help identify backup failures or storage capacity constraints promptly. Consider implementing logging and auditing to track backup and recovery activities, ensuring accountability and compliance. Backup and recovery best practices in VirtualBox play a critical role in maintaining the availability and integrity of virtual machines and data. By following these guidelines, organizations can minimize the risk of data loss, reduce downtime, and ensure business continuity in virtualized environments. Effective backup and recovery strategies are integral to a comprehensive IT infrastructure plan, safeguarding against unexpected challenges and ensuring that virtualization technology delivers its full potential.

Chapter 8: Advanced VirtualBox Features

Exploring advanced features of VirtualBox opens up a world of possibilities for optimizing your virtualization experience. While VirtualBox is known for its user-friendly interface and straightforward setup, it also offers a range of advanced features that can enhance your virtual machine management and performance. One such feature is the ability to create and manage multiple virtual networks within VirtualBox. Virtual networks allow you to establish isolated network environments for your virtual machines, mimicking complex network setups for testing or development purposes. By configuring virtual networks, you can simulate scenarios like VLANs, subnets, and firewall rules to test network-related configurations and security measures. VirtualBox provides a network editor tool that makes it easy to create and manage these virtual networks, giving you fine-grained control over network settings. Another advanced feature of VirtualBox is the capability to create and manage virtual machine groups. Virtual machine groups allow you to organize and control multiple virtual machines simultaneously. For example, you can group virtual machines that belong to a specific project, department, or purpose and apply group-level settings and operations. This feature streamlines management tasks, making it efficient to start, stop, or modify settings for a group of virtual machines at once. Snapshots, a well-known feature in VirtualBox, have advanced capabilities that go beyond basic point-in-time captures of virtual machines. With snapshots, you can create branching snapshots, which enable you to create multiple diverging paths for your virtual machine's state. This is particularly useful for testing different scenarios within the same virtual machine. Branching snapshots allow you to explore various configurations and return to different points in time without affecting the original state of the virtual machine. VirtualBox also supports storage enhancements, such as the ability to use raw disk access for virtual machines. Raw disk access allows virtual machines to interact directly with physical hard disks or partitions, providing the potential for high-performance and compatibility with existing data. This feature is beneficial when you need to run virtual machines that require direct access to specific storage devices, such as those used in data recovery or forensic analysis. In addition to raw disk access, VirtualBox offers the option to create dynamically allocated or fixed-size virtual hard disks. Dynamically allocated disks start small and grow as needed, consuming only the space necessary for the data stored within the virtual machine. Fixed-size disks, on the other hand, allocate the entire disk space upfront, providing consistent performance but using more host storage. Choosing the appropriate disk type depends on your specific requirements and resource availability. For advanced users and developers, VirtualBox supports remote display and control of virtual machines through the VirtualBox Remote Desktop Extension (VRDE). VRDE allows you to access virtual machines over a network connection, providing a remote desktop-like experience. This feature is valuable when you need to manage and interact with virtual machines on remote hosts or within headless server environments. Performance optimization is a key consideration when using VirtualBox for resource-intensive workloads. VirtualBox provides a range of features to fine-tune the performance of virtual machines. For instance, you can enable hardware virtualization extensions (VT-x/AMD-V) for better performance and compatibility with 64-bit guest operating systems. You can also allocate more CPU cores and memory to virtual machines to improve their performance. Additionally, VirtualBox offers options for adjusting virtual machine execution priority and limiting resource usage to prevent overcommitment of host resources. Advanced users may leverage command-line interfaces (CLIs) and scripting to automate VirtualBox operations. VirtualBox provides a powerful CLI called VBoxManage, allowing you to create, configure, and manage virtual machines programmatically. Using scripts and automation tools, you can orchestrate complex workflows, deploy virtual machines at scale, and integrate VirtualBox into larger IT ecosystems. VirtualBox's extensibility is another advanced feature that enables you to extend its capabilities. VirtualBox supports various extensions, including VirtualBox Extension Packs and guest additions. Extension Packs provide additional functionality, such as USB 2.0/3.0 support, remote desktop protocols, and encryption features. Guest additions, on the other hand, enhance the integration between the host and guest operating systems. They enable features like seamless window integration, improved graphics performance, and shared clipboard functionality. VirtualBox's modular architecture allows you to install and manage these extensions as needed. Advanced users can take advantage of VirtualBox's support for multiple virtualization formats. VirtualBox supports the import and export of virtual machines in various formats, including OVF (Open Virtualization Format) and OVA (Open Virtualization Appliance). This flexibility makes it easy to migrate virtual machines between different virtualization platforms or share them with others. For organizations with specific security and access control requirements, VirtualBox offers advanced features for user and group management. You can define roles and permissions to control who can create, modify, or access virtual machines. This feature is valuable in environments where strict access control and auditing are necessary. VirtualBox also supports seamless integration with third-party applications and services. You can enhance VirtualBox's functionality by integrating it with backup solutions, monitoring tools, or cloud services. This extensibility allows you to tailor VirtualBox to your organization's unique needs and workflows. In addition to its advanced features, VirtualBox has a vibrant community and ecosystem. You can find a wealth of resources, including forums, documentation, and third-party plugins and extensions, to further enhance your VirtualBox experience. Regularly updating VirtualBox to the latest version is essential to benefit from bug fixes, performance improvements, and new features. VirtualBox's active development community ensures that it remains a competitive and reliable virtualization platform. In summary, exploring the advanced features of VirtualBox opens up opportunities to optimize virtual machine management, enhance performance, and streamline complex tasks. Whether you are a seasoned virtualization professional or new to virtualization, VirtualBox's advanced capabilities offer valuable tools and options to meet your needs and achieve your goals. By harnessing these features effectively, you can maximize the potential of VirtualBox and make it an integral part of your IT infrastructure.

Using USB and Remote Desktop features in VirtualBox expands the capabilities of your virtual machines, making them more versatile and accessible. VirtualBox provides robust support for USB devices, allowing you to connect USB peripherals to your virtual machines seamlessly. This feature is particularly valuable when you need to interact with hardware devices within your virtualized environment. To enable USB support, you must first install the VirtualBox Extension Pack, which includes the necessary USB drivers and support for USB 2.0 and USB 3.0 devices. Once the Extension Pack is installed, you can configure USB device filters to control which USB devices are automatically passed through to your virtual machine when they are connected to your host system. USB device filters allow you to specify criteria such as device type, vendor ID, product ID, and more. This level of granularity ensures that only the desired USB devices are available to your virtual machines. When a USB device is connected to your host system, VirtualBox checks if it matches any of the configured filters and, if so, makes it available to the virtual machine. USB device pass-through is useful for a wide range of scenarios, such as using USB printers, scanners, external storage devices, cameras, and more within your virtual machines. For example, if you have a Windows virtual machine running on a Linux host and need to print a document, you can connect a USB printer to your host system, and VirtualBox will make it available to the virtual machine. This seamless integration of USB devices enhances the flexibility and functionality of your virtualized environment. In addition to USB support, VirtualBox offers powerful Remote Desktop features that enable you to access and control your virtual machines remotely. This is particularly beneficial when you need to manage virtual machines that are running on headless servers or remote hosts. VirtualBox provides two main mechanisms for remote desktop access: VRDP (VirtualBox Remote Desktop Protocol) and RDP (Remote Desktop Protocol). VRDP is VirtualBox's native remote desktop protocol, designed specifically for accessing virtual machines hosted by VirtualBox. It offers features like secure authentication, encryption, and session management. To enable VRDP, you must configure it in the virtual machine's settings and specify the desired port for remote desktop connections. Once configured, you can use a remote desktop client that supports VRDP to connect to your virtual machine and control it as if you were physically present. RDP, on the other hand, is a widely used remote desktop protocol developed by Microsoft. VirtualBox supports RDP as well, allowing you to connect to your virtual machines using RDP clients like Microsoft's Remote Desktop Connection or third-party alternatives. To enable RDP for a virtual machine, you need to install the VirtualBox Extension Pack and enable the VRDP extension. Afterward, you can configure RDP settings in the virtual machine's properties, including authentication and encryption options. Both VRDP and RDP provide secure and efficient remote desktop access to your virtual machines. They allow you to perform tasks like configuring settings, installing software, and troubleshooting issues without physically accessing the host system or requiring a graphical user interface on the host. Remote desktop access is especially valuable in server environments where graphical interfaces are not necessary or practical. By using remote desktop features, you can manage virtual machines on headless servers, reduce downtime, and efficiently administer your virtualized infrastructure. It's important to note that when using remote desktop access, you should consider security best practices to protect your virtual machines and data. This includes using strong authentication methods, applying encryption for data transfer, and restricting access to authorized users. Additionally, regularly updating VirtualBox and its extensions helps ensure that you have the latest security patches and enhancements for remote desktop functionality. USB support and remote desktop access in

VirtualBox enhance the usability and manageability of virtual machines, whether they are used for development, testing, or production purposes. These features extend the reach of virtualization technology, allowing you to leverage its benefits in diverse environments and use cases. Whether you need to connect USB devices seamlessly to your virtual machines or remotely administer them without direct physical access, VirtualBox provides the tools and flexibility to meet your requirements. By mastering USB and remote desktop features, you can unlock the full potential of your virtualized infrastructure and streamline your virtual machine management tasks effectively and securely.

Chapter 9: Performance Optimization and Troubleshooting

Optimizing virtual machine performance is a crucial aspect of managing a virtualized environment effectively. Virtualization technology offers significant benefits, such as resource consolidation, scalability, and flexibility. However, achieving optimal performance for virtual machines requires careful planning, monitoring, and tuning. One of the first steps in optimizing performance is to allocate appropriate resources to each virtual machine. Resource allocation includes CPU cores, memory, storage, and network bandwidth. Underallocating resources can lead to sluggish performance, while overallocating can result in resource contention and inefficiency. Balancing resource allocation is essential to ensure that each virtual machine has enough capacity to run its workloads smoothly. To achieve this balance, monitor resource utilization regularly and adjust allocation as needed. Modern virtualization platforms, like VMware, Hyper-V, and VirtualBox, provide dynamic resource allocation features that allow virtual machines to use additional resources when they are available. These features can help maximize resource utilization without manual intervention. Another key consideration for performance optimization is storage configuration. Storage plays a significant role in virtual machine performance, affecting boot times, application responsiveness, and data access speeds. Utilize fast and reliable storage solutions, such as solid-state drives (SSDs) or network-attached storage (NAS), to reduce storage-related bottlenecks. Implementing storage virtualization technologies like storage area networks (SANs) or network-attached storage (NAS) can also improve storage performance and scalability. Furthermore, consider using storage technologies that support features like thin provisioning, deduplication, and compression to optimize storage utilization and reduce I/O overhead. I/O optimization is crucial for virtual machine performance. Distributed storage systems and hybrid storage solutions can distribute I/O operations across multiple disks or storage devices, enhancing I/O performance and fault tolerance. Storage caching mechanisms, such as read and write caching, can accelerate I/O operations by caching frequently accessed data. These caching mechanisms reduce the need to fetch data from slower storage devices, resulting in faster application response times. Network performance is another critical aspect of virtual machine optimization. Ensure that your network infrastructure, including switches, routers, and network adapters, supports the required bandwidth and low-latency communication. Utilize virtual LANs (VLANs) and quality of service (QoS) configurations to segment network traffic and prioritize critical workloads. By segmenting traffic and prioritizing essential applications, you can prevent network congestion and ensure reliable communication between virtual machines. Monitoring and management tools play a vital role in optimizing virtual machine performance. Leverage performance monitoring and analysis tools to identify performance bottlenecks and resource utilization patterns. Tools like vSphere Performance Charts for VMware, Resource Monitor for Hyper-V, and VirtualBox's built-in monitoring capabilities provide insights into CPU, memory, network, and storage usage. These tools help administrators identify performance anomalies, track trends, and make informed decisions to improve virtual machine performance. Proactive monitoring also enables administrators to identify potential issues before they impact virtual machine performance adversely. Capacity planning is essential for optimizing virtual machine performance in the long term. Understand the growth trends and resource requirements of your virtualized workloads. By forecasting future resource needs, you can allocate resources more efficiently and avoid resource shortages. Capacity planning also helps you make informed decisions about hardware upgrades or scaling out your virtualized infrastructure. Virtual machine consolidation is an effective strategy to optimize resource usage and improve performance. By consolidating multiple virtual machines onto a single physical host, you can reduce hardware and operational costs while improving resource utilization. Virtual machine density should be carefully managed to avoid resource contention, so consider factors like resource demands, workload characteristics, and redundancy requirements when planning consolidation. Resource pools and load balancing are advanced techniques for optimizing virtual machine performance. Resource pools allow you to group virtual machines with similar resource requirements and allocate resources to the pool as a whole. Load balancing distributes virtual machines across multiple physical hosts to distribute workloads evenly and ensure resource availability. These techniques help maximize resource utilization and performance while maintaining high availability. Performance tuning involves optimizing the virtualization platform itself to enhance virtual machine performance. This may include adjusting hypervisor settings, configuring host-level optimizations, or fine-tuning virtual machine settings. For example, optimizing CPU scheduling policies, enabling hardware-assisted virtualization, and adjusting memory ballooning settings can improve virtual machine performance significantly. Always consider security implications when making performance optimizations, as certain configurations may introduce vulnerabilities. Performance benchmarking is a valuable practice for evaluating virtual machine performance and identifying areas for improvement. Benchmarking tools, like SPECvirt for measuring virtualization performance or industry-standard tools like Iometer, can provide baseline performance metrics. Compare benchmark results against industry standards and best practices to assess the effectiveness of performance optimizations. Regularly review and update virtual machine templates and golden images. Templates and images serve as the foundation for creating new virtual machines. By keeping templates and images up-to-date with the latest patches, updates, and optimized configurations, you ensure that newly provisioned virtual machines start with optimal settings and security. Managing virtual machine workloads efficiently is crucial for performance optimization. Load balancing and workload migration tools can help distribute workloads evenly across the virtualized infrastructure. These tools automatically move virtual machines to hosts with available resources, preventing resource contention and ensuring consistent performance. Performance troubleshooting is an ongoing process in virtualized environments. When performance issues arise, use diagnostic tools and logs to pinpoint the root causes. Address performance bottlenecks by adjusting resource allocation, optimizing configurations, or applying patches and updates. Collaborate with system administrators, network engineers, and application developers to resolve complex performance issues that span multiple layers of the infrastructure. Performance optimization in virtualized environments is a continuous effort that requires a deep understanding of the virtualization platform, hardware, and workloads. By following best practices, monitoring resource utilization, and staying informed about virtualization technologies, administrators can ensure that virtual machines perform at their best. Ultimately, a well-optimized virtualized infrastructure provides the agility, scalability, and efficiency needed to support diverse workloads and meet the demands of modern IT environments.

Troubleshooting common issues in VirtualBox is an essential skill for maintaining a stable and efficient virtualized environment. VirtualBox is a powerful virtualization platform that provides a wide range of features and capabilities. However, like any software, it can encounter problems that require investigation and resolution. This chapter explores some of the most common issues that VirtualBox users may encounter and provides guidance on how to troubleshoot and resolve them. One frequent issue is virtual machine instability or crashes. Virtual machines can become unstable for various reasons, including incompatible configurations, resource constraints, or software conflicts. To troubleshoot this issue, start by reviewing the virtual machine's settings and comparing them to the recommended configurations for the guest operating system. Ensure that you have allocated sufficient CPU cores, memory, and storage to the virtual machine. Check for conflicts with other software running on the host system, such as antivirus programs or third-party virtualization tools. Sometimes, updating VirtualBox to the latest version or applying guest additions and extension packs can resolve stability issues. Another common problem is networking-related issues within virtual machines. These issues can manifest as problems with internet connectivity, network shares, or DNS resolution. To troubleshoot network problems, start by verifying the virtual machine's network settings. Ensure that the virtual machine is using the correct network adapter type and that it is connected to the appropriate virtual network. Check the network configuration within the guest operating system to ensure it is set up correctly, including IP addressing, subnet masks, and gateway settings. If the virtual machine relies on DNS resolution, confirm that DNS servers are configured correctly in the guest OS. Sometimes, resetting the virtual machine's network adapter or restarting network services within the guest can resolve network issues. Performance problems are another common concern when using VirtualBox. Virtual machines may experience sluggishness or resource contention, leading to degraded performance. To troubleshoot performance issues, monitor the virtual machine's resource utilization using tools like Task Manager (on Windows) or top (on Linux). Identify if any resource, such as CPU, memory, or disk I/O, is consistently under heavy load. Check for resource overcommitment on the host system, which can lead to contention. Adjust the resource allocation for the virtual machine, if necessary, to ensure it has adequate resources. Consider using VirtualBox's built-in performance monitoring and logging features to gain insights into resource utilization trends. Storage-related problems can also occur, resulting in data corruption or virtual machine boot failures. Troubleshooting storage issues involves examining the virtual hard disk configuration, file system integrity, and storage device compatibility. Check the virtual hard disk's settings, such as storage format (e.g., VDI, VHD, VMDK) and disk size. Ensure that the virtual hard disk file is not corrupted, and consider creating backups or snapshots before attempting any fixes. Inside the virtual machine, use disk checking utilities to verify and repair file system integrity. If a virtual hard disk has insufficient space, you may need to resize it or allocate additional storage. Sometimes, storage performance can be improved by using a different virtual hard disk format or optimizing the storage controller type in the virtual machine's settings. Audio and video issues can also affect the virtual machine's usability. Common problems include no audio output, distorted sound, or video rendering glitches. Troubleshooting audio and video issues involves checking the virtual machine's audio and video settings, as well as guest additions installation. Ensure that the virtual machine has the necessary audio and video drivers installed by installing guest additions or extension packs. Verify that the virtual machine's audio and video settings match the host's specifications and that there are no conflicts with other software or hardware. If audio or video problems persist, try updating the virtual machine's guest additions to the latest version. In some cases, disabling or re-enabling audio or video support within the virtual machine's settings may resolve issues. USB device compatibility issues can occur when attempting to connect USB devices to the virtual machine. If a USB device is not recognized or does not function correctly within the virtual machine, start by confirming that the device is properly connected to the host system and is compatible with VirtualBox. Check the virtual machine's USB settings to ensure that USB support is enabled and that the device is selected for passthrough. Sometimes, installing or updating VirtualBox Extension Packs may provide better USB support. Ensure that the guest operating system within the virtual machine has the necessary USB drivers installed. If USB device issues persist, consider testing the device on a different USB port or host system to rule out hardware problems. Snapshot and cloning problems can occur when attempting to create or manage snapshots and clones of virtual machines. Snapshots are essential for preserving virtual machine states, but issues may arise when creating, reverting to, or deleting snapshots. Troubleshooting snapshot issues involves checking for available storage space, ensuring that the virtual machine is in a stable state, and verifying that the snapshot hierarchy is not excessively complex.

Complex snapshot chains can lead to performance problems and increased risk of data corruption. Cloning issues may arise when creating duplicate virtual machines for testing or backup purposes. Ensure that you have enough storage space to accommodate the cloned virtual machine. If the cloning process fails, review the error messages and log files for more information about the problem. Occasionally, issues with VirtualBox itself may occur, such as crashes, freezes, or errors during installation or startup. To address these problems, consider updating VirtualBox to the latest version, as newer releases often include bug fixes and stability improvements. Check the VirtualBox forums, user documentation, and bug tracker for known issues and solutions. If you encounter frequent crashes or stability problems, consider the possibility of conflicts with other software or hardware on the host system. In such cases, troubleshooting may involve identifying and mitigating conflicts. Sometimes, problems with VirtualBox can be related to the host operating system's configuration or security settings. Firewalls, antivirus software, or restrictive permissions may interfere with VirtualBox's functionality. Ensure that VirtualBox has the necessary permissions and exemptions within the host operating system to operate smoothly. If you experience problems during VirtualBox installation or startup, review error messages and consult the user manual or online resources for troubleshooting guidance. In summary, troubleshooting common issues in VirtualBox requires a systematic approach to identify and resolve problems effectively. By examining virtual machine settings, resource allocation, hardware compatibility, and guest operating system configurations, administrators can address stability, networking, performance, storage, audio, video, USB, snapshot, cloning, and platform-specific issues. Regularly updating VirtualBox and its components, including guest additions and extension packs, is essential to benefit from bug fixes and improvements. Additionally, staying informed about VirtualBox's community resources, forums, and support channels can provide valuable insights and solutions to common problems. By mastering the art of troubleshooting in VirtualBox, administrators can maintain a robust and reliable virtualized environment that meets the demands of diverse workloads and user needs.

Chapter 10: Security Best Practices for VirtualBox

Virtual machine security is a paramount concern in today's computing landscape, where virtualization technologies play a central role in data centers, cloud environments, and development workflows. Securing virtual machines is essential to protect sensitive data, prevent unauthorized access, and mitigate the risk of cyberattacks. This chapter explores the core security principles and best practices that every virtualization administrator should consider when managing virtual machines. Understanding the security implications of virtualization is the first step towards effective virtual machine security. Virtualization introduces new attack surfaces and potential vulnerabilities that must be addressed. Virtual machines share the same physical hardware resources and may run on the same host, creating opportunities for lateral movement and unauthorized access. As a result, administrators must implement robust security measures to safeguard virtualized environments. One of the fundamental aspects of virtual machine security is isolation. Isolation ensures that virtual machines are separated from each other and the host system, reducing the risk of data leakage or unauthorized access. Virtualization platforms provide features like hardware-level isolation, resource allocation, and network segmentation to achieve this goal. Isolation is particularly critical in multi-tenant environments, such as cloud computing, where multiple users or organizations share the same infrastructure. Implementing strong access controls and authentication mechanisms is essential for virtual machine security. Authentication ensures that only authorized users or systems can access and manage virtual machines. Use strong, unique passwords or passphrase policies for administrative access, and consider implementing multi-factor authentication (MFA) to add an extra layer of security. Leverage role-based access control (RBAC) to assign permissions and restrict access to specific virtual machines and resources based on user roles and responsibilities. Regularly review and audit user accounts and permissions to identify and revoke unnecessary privileges. Patch management is a cornerstone of virtual machine security. Just as with physical servers, virtual machines are susceptible to software vulnerabilities that can be exploited by attackers. Ensure that virtual machine operating systems, hypervisors, and guest additions are kept up-to-date with the latest security patches and updates. Implement a patch management strategy that includes regular vulnerability assessments, testing, and timely patch deployment. Security policies and hardening guidelines should be established and enforced consistently across all virtual machines. Adopt security baselines, such as those provided by organizations like the Center for Internet Security (CIS) or vendor-specific guidelines, to harden virtual machine configurations. These baselines include recommendations for disabling unnecessary services, enabling firewall rules, and configuring security settings. Apply host-based firewalls or security groups to control network traffic to and from virtual machines. Incorporate intrusion detection and prevention systems (IDPS) to monitor and alert on suspicious network activities. Implement endpoint protection solutions, such as antivirus and anti-malware software, within virtual machines to detect and mitigate threats. Data encryption is crucial for protecting sensitive information within virtual machines. Implement encryption for data at rest and data in transit. Encrypt virtual hard disks, databases, and sensitive files to prevent unauthorized access to data stored within virtual machines. Utilize encrypted communication protocols, such as TLS/SSL, for data transmission between virtual machines and external systems. Consider using virtual private networks (VPNs) or encrypted tunnels to secure network traffic between virtual machines and remote locations. Virtual machine backups are essential for data recovery and business continuity, but they must also be protected. Ensure that backup copies of virtual machines are securely stored and encrypted to prevent data exposure in case of theft or unauthorized access. Implement access controls and authentication for backup systems and repositories. Test backup and recovery procedures regularly to verify data integrity and the ability to restore virtual machines in case of data loss or system compromise. Regularly audit and monitor virtual machine activity and resource usage to detect and respond to security incidents. Leverage logging and monitoring solutions that capture events and activities within virtual machines, as well as at the hypervisor level. Set up alerting mechanisms to notify administrators of suspicious activities or deviations from normal behavior. Incorporate security information and event management (SIEM) systems to aggregate and analyze log data from virtual machines and host systems. Develop an incident response plan that outlines procedures for identifying, mitigating, and recovering from security incidents. Define roles and responsibilities within the incident response team and establish communication channels for reporting and escalating incidents. Regularly conduct tabletop exercises and simulations to ensure that the incident response plan is effective and well-practiced. Virtual machine snapshots are useful for capturing the state of a virtual machine at a specific point in time, but they should be managed carefully from a security perspective. Snapshots may contain sensitive data or configurations that could be exposed if the snapshot is compromised. Apply access controls to snapshots and limit access to authorized personnel. Implement encryption for snapshot files to protect their contents. Regularly delete unnecessary snapshots to reduce the attack surface and prevent unauthorized access. Consider compliance requirements and regulations that apply to virtualized environments. Certain industries and organizations must adhere to specific security standards and compliance frameworks, such as the Payment Card Industry Data Security Standard (PCI DSS) or the Health Insurance Portability and Accountability Act (HIPAA). Ensure that virtual machine security measures align with the relevant compliance requirements and undergo regular audits or assessments to demonstrate compliance. Education and training are essential components of virtual machine security. Raise awareness among virtualization administrators, users, and stakeholders about security risks, best practices, and policies. Provide training on secure configuration, incident response, and security awareness to ensure that personnel can recognize and respond to security threats effectively. Stay informed about emerging threats and vulnerabilities in virtualization technology. Regularly monitor security advisories and updates from virtualization vendors and security organizations. Participate in the virtualization community and forums to share knowledge and best practices with peers. Collaborate with other IT and security teams to align virtual machine security with the overall organizational security strategy. Virtual machine security is an ongoing effort that requires vigilance and adaptability in the face of evolving threats. By following these security essentials, administrators can minimize risks, protect sensitive data, and maintain the integrity and availability of virtualized environments. Ultimately, a well-secured virtual machine infrastructure serves as a strong foundation for achieving operational efficiency and supporting the diverse needs of modern IT environments.

Implementing robust security measures in VirtualBox is crucial for safeguarding virtualized environments from potential threats and vulnerabilities. VirtualBox, like other virtualization platforms, introduces unique security challenges and opportunities. By following best practices and security guidelines, administrators can ensure that virtual machines running in VirtualBox remain protected and resilient. One of the first steps in securing VirtualBox is to keep the software up-to-date. Regularly apply updates and patches to the VirtualBox software itself, as well as any extensions and guest additions. Updates often include security fixes and improvements that address known vulnerabilities. Check for new releases and advisories from the VirtualBox vendor, and establish a patch management process to keep the software current. Virtual machine images should be created from clean and trusted sources. When building virtual machines, use official operating system images and installation media obtained from reputable sources. Avoid using pre-built virtual machine images from unverified or unknown sources, as they may contain malware or compromised configurations. Additionally, scan and verify the integrity of the installation media or images before deploying virtual machines. Isolation is a fundamental security principle in VirtualBox. Ensure that virtual machines are isolated from each other and the host system. Use separate virtual networks and network segments to segment traffic and isolate virtual machines from one another. Leverage VirtualBox's network configurations to implement firewall rules and access controls to restrict communication between virtual machines. Disable unnecessary hardware devices and virtual hardware features that are not needed for a particular virtual machine. By limiting the attack surface, you reduce the risk of exploitation through vulnerable components. Resource allocation is a critical aspect of security. Allocate resources such as CPU cores, memory, and storage to virtual machines based on their actual needs. Overallocating resources can lead to resource contention and security risks, while underallocating can impact performance. Monitor resource utilization regularly and adjust allocations accordingly. Encryption is essential for protecting data within virtual machines. Implement encryption for virtual hard disks to prevent unauthorized access to data at rest. VirtualBox supports the use of encrypted virtual hard disks in various formats, such as VHD, VDI, and VMDK. Ensure that sensitive data stored within virtual machines is encrypted using encryption technologies available within the guest operating system. Encrypt communication between virtual machines and external systems by using secure protocols like TLS/SSL for data in transit. Implementing secure passwords and access controls is paramount for VirtualBox security. Utilize strong and unique passwords for administrative access to VirtualBox and the host system. Consider implementing multi-factor authentication (MFA) for enhanced access security. Leverage role-based access control (RBAC) mechanisms to assign permissions and restrict access to specific virtual machines and features based on user roles and responsibilities. Regularly review and audit user accounts and permissions to minimize security risks. Security policies and hardening guidelines should be established and consistently applied to virtual machines. Adopt security baselines, such as those provided by organizations like the Center for Internet

Security (CIS), that provide recommendations for securing operating systems and applications. Harden the configurations of virtual machines by disabling unnecessary services, minimizing attack surfaces, and applying security patches and updates. Implement host-based firewalls or security groups to control incoming and outgoing network traffic to virtual machines. Intrusion detection and prevention systems (IDPS) can be used to monitor network traffic for suspicious activities and potential threats. Endpoint protection solutions, including antivirus and anti-malware software, should be installed within virtual machines to detect and mitigate security threats. Data backups are a crucial component of security. Regularly back up virtual machine data to ensure business continuity and disaster recovery capabilities. Store backup copies securely and implement access controls and encryption to protect backup data from unauthorized access. Test backup and recovery procedures to verify data integrity and the ability to restore virtual machines in case of data loss or compromise. Virtual machine snapshots are a valuable tool for capturing and preserving the state of a virtual machine at a specific point in time. However, manage snapshots carefully from a security perspective. Snapshots may contain sensitive data or configurations that could be exposed if the snapshot is compromised. Apply access controls to snapshots and limit access to authorized personnel. Implement encryption for snapshot files to protect their contents. Regularly delete unnecessary snapshots to reduce the attack surface and prevent unauthorized access. Regularly monitor and audit virtual machine activity and resource utilization. Implement logging and monitoring solutions that capture events and activities within virtual machines and at the hypervisor level. Set up alerting mechanisms to notify administrators of suspicious activities or deviations from normal behavior. Incorporate security information and event management (SIEM) systems to aggregate and analyze log data from virtual machines and host systems. Develop an incident response plan to outline procedures for identifying, mitigating, and recovering from security incidents. Define roles and responsibilities within the incident response team and establish communication channels for reporting and escalating incidents. Conduct regular tabletop exercises and simulations to ensure that the incident response plan is effective and well-practiced. Security compliance is essential for organizations that must adhere to specific security standards and regulations. Ensure that virtual machine security measures align with the relevant compliance requirements and undergo regular audits or assessments to demonstrate compliance. Education and training play a crucial role in virtual machine security. Raise awareness among virtualization administrators, users, and stakeholders about security risks, best practices, and policies. Provide training on secure configuration, incident response, and security awareness to ensure that personnel can recognize and respond to security threats effectively. Stay informed about emerging threats and vulnerabilities in VirtualBox and virtualization technology in general. Monitor security advisories, updates, and industry news to stay ahead of potential security risks. Collaborate with other IT and security teams to align VirtualBox security with the overall organizational security strategy. Security in VirtualBox is an ongoing effort that requires continuous attention and adaptation to evolving threats. By following these security measures, administrators can create a secure virtualized environment that protects data, minimizes risks, and supports the organization's goals and objectives. A well-secured VirtualBox environment serves as a foundation for reliable and resilient virtualization operations.

BOOK 3
ADVANCED VIRTUALIZATION WITH PARALLELS DESKTOP
OPTIMIZING FOR PRODUCTIVITY AND PERFORMANCE

ROB BOTWRIGHT

Chapter 1: Introduction to Parallels Desktop

Understanding Virtualization with Parallels Desktop is essential for gaining insights into this powerful virtualization software designed for macOS. Parallels Desktop allows Mac users to run multiple operating systems, including Windows and Linux, alongside macOS on their Mac computers. Virtualization, in this context, enables the simultaneous operation of multiple operating systems on a single physical machine. This chapter explores the key concepts, features, and use cases of Parallels Desktop, providing a foundational understanding of this technology. At its core, Parallels Desktop is a virtualization platform that leverages hardware virtualization technology to create virtual machines (VMs). These VMs are isolated instances of operating systems that run alongside macOS. Parallels Desktop provides a user-friendly interface and seamless integration with macOS, making it accessible to a wide range of users. One of the primary advantages of using Parallels Desktop is the ability to run Windows on a Mac without the need for a separate physical PC. This capability is particularly useful for users who require Windows-specific applications for work or personal use. With Parallels Desktop, users can switch between macOS and Windows seamlessly, sharing files and resources between the two operating systems. Another key benefit of Parallels Desktop is its support for running multiple virtual machines concurrently. This means users can run not only Windows but also other operating systems like Linux distributions, macOS versions, or even experimental OS builds. Each virtual machine operates independently, allowing users to perform different tasks or run various software in isolated environments. Parallels Desktop offers a range of features that enhance the virtualization experience. One such feature is Coherence mode, which allows Windows applications to run side by side with macOS applications, making it appear as if they are running directly on the Mac desktop. Users can launch Windows applications from the macOS Dock and switch between them seamlessly. Parallels Desktop also includes features like Snapshots, which enable users to take snapshots of virtual machines at specific points in time. These snapshots serve as backups and can be used to revert to a previous state of the virtual machine in case of errors or issues. Performance optimization is a critical aspect of virtualization with Parallels Desktop. To ensure smooth operation, users should allocate an adequate amount of CPU cores, memory, and disk space to each virtual machine. Adjusting these resources based on the virtual machine's requirements can significantly impact performance. Parallels Desktop also provides an option to allocate more graphics memory to virtual machines, which can be beneficial for running graphics-intensive applications or games. Networking is another important consideration when working with Parallels Desktop. Users can configure network settings for virtual machines to ensure proper communication with the host system and external networks. Parallels Desktop supports various network modes, including bridged, shared, and host-only networking, allowing users to tailor network configurations to their needs. Integration with macOS is a standout feature of Parallels Desktop. Users can easily drag and drop files between the Mac desktop and virtual machines. Clipboard sharing enables copying and pasting text and files between macOS and virtual machines seamlessly. Furthermore, users can share folders between the host macOS system and virtual machines, simplifying file access and management. Parallels Desktop also offers support for USB devices, allowing users to connect and use USB peripherals within virtual machines. Additionally, the software provides a feature called Coherence mode, which integrates Windows applications into the macOS environment. This mode enables users to run Windows applications alongside their macOS apps, providing a unified desktop experience. Parallels Desktop supports a wide range of operating systems, making it a versatile virtualization solution. Users can create virtual machines with various guest operating systems, including different versions of Windows, Linux distributions, and even macOS itself. This flexibility makes Parallels Desktop suitable for a variety of use cases, from running legacy software to testing different operating systems and software configurations. Security is a crucial aspect of virtualization with Parallels Desktop. Users should ensure that their virtual machines are adequately protected by implementing security best practices. This includes keeping the guest operating systems and software within virtual machines up to date with security patches and updates. Users should also employ strong, unique passwords for virtual machine accounts and consider implementing encryption for sensitive data stored within virtual machines. Regular backups of virtual machines are recommended to safeguard against data loss or corruption. Parallels Desktop provides users with the ability to create and manage snapshots of virtual machines, which serve as backups that can be used to restore a virtual machine to a previous state. These snapshots can be a valuable tool for recovering from errors or issues within virtual machines. In summary, understanding virtualization with Parallels Desktop opens up a world of possibilities for Mac users. By harnessing the power of virtualization, individuals and organizations can run multiple operating systems on a single Mac, improving productivity, flexibility, and compatibility. Whether it's running Windows applications, testing software configurations, or exploring different operating systems, Parallels Desktop provides a seamless and user-friendly virtualization solution for macOS users. With its diverse feature set, performance optimization options, and integration with macOS, Parallels Desktop offers a robust virtualization experience for both beginners and experienced users alike.

Exploring the features of Parallels Desktop unveils a wide array of capabilities that enhance the virtualization experience on macOS. Parallels Desktop is a versatile virtualization software that enables users to run multiple operating systems seamlessly on their Mac computers. This chapter delves into the various features and functionalities that make Parallels Desktop a popular choice among Mac users. One of the standout features of Parallels Desktop is its support for running Windows on a Mac, providing users with the ability to run Windows applications side by side with macOS applications. This feature is invaluable for individuals and businesses that rely on Windows-specific software for various tasks. Parallels Desktop allows users to install and run different versions of Windows, including older legacy versions and the latest Windows 10 or Windows 11. In addition to Windows, Parallels Desktop supports a wide range of guest operating systems, such as various Linux distributions, macOS versions, and even experimental or niche operating systems. This versatility makes it a suitable choice for a diverse set of use cases, from software development and testing to running specialized applications. Coherence mode is a unique feature of Parallels Desktop that enhances the integration of Windows applications with macOS. In Coherence mode, Windows applications appear as if they are running natively on the Mac desktop, seamlessly blending with macOS apps. Users can launch Windows applications directly from the macOS Dock, switch between them effortlessly, and even use macOS gestures within these applications. Parallels Desktop's Coherence mode provides a unified and user-friendly computing experience. Snapshots are a valuable feature for virtual machine management within Parallels Desktop. With snapshots, users can capture the state of a virtual machine at a specific point in time. These snapshots serve as backups and can be used to revert a virtual machine to a previous state if errors or issues arise. Snapshots provide peace of mind by allowing users to experiment and make changes within virtual machines without the fear of permanent data loss. Resource allocation and performance optimization are critical aspects of virtualization, and Parallels Desktop offers various options to fine-tune virtual machine performance. Users can allocate CPU cores, memory, and disk space to virtual machines based on their specific requirements. This flexibility ensures that virtual machines have the necessary resources to operate smoothly while preventing resource contention with the host system. Parallels Desktop also provides an option to allocate more graphics memory to virtual machines, which is beneficial for graphics-intensive applications and games. Networking capabilities in Parallels Desktop enable users to configure virtual machine network settings to meet their needs. Users can choose from different network modes, including bridged, shared, and host-only networking, depending on the desired level of network isolation and connectivity. This flexibility allows users to create network configurations that suit their specific requirements. Integration with macOS is a hallmark of Parallels Desktop. Users can easily move files between the Mac desktop and virtual machines by dragging and dropping. Clipboard sharing enables seamless copying and pasting of text and files between macOS and virtual machines. Moreover, users can share folders between the host macOS system and virtual machines, simplifying file access and data exchange.

Parallels Desktop also supports USB devices, allowing users to connect and use USB peripherals within virtual machines. Additionally, the software provides a Unity mode, similar to Coherence mode but designed for Linux virtual machines. Unity mode seamlessly integrates Linux applications with the macOS environment, enhancing the user experience for those running Linux-based software. Security is a paramount consideration when using Parallels Desktop for virtualization. Users should ensure that their virtual machines are adequately protected. This involves keeping the guest operating systems and software within virtual machines up to date with security patches and updates. Strong and unique passwords should be employed for virtual machine accounts, and users may consider implementing encryption for sensitive data stored within virtual machines. Regular backups of virtual machines are recommended to safeguard against data loss or corruption. Parallels Desktop provides users with the ability to create and manage snapshots of virtual machines, which serve as backups that can be used to restore a virtual machine to a previous state. These snapshots can be a valuable tool for recovering from errors or issues within virtual machines. In summary, exploring the features of Parallels Desktop reveals a robust virtualization solution for Mac users. Its ability to seamlessly run Windows and other operating systems on a Mac, combined with features like Coherence mode, snapshots, and performance optimization options, makes it a versatile tool for various use cases. Parallels Desktop's integration with macOS and support for a wide range of guest operating systems enhance its usability and flexibility. Security considerations, including updates, strong passwords, and backups, are essential to ensure the safe and reliable operation of virtual machines within Parallels Desktop. Overall, Parallels Desktop empowers Mac users to harness the full potential of virtualization for productivity, software testing, and exploration, making it a valuable addition to the macOS ecosystem.

Chapter 2: Installing Parallels Desktop and Guest Tools

Preparing your Mac for Parallels Desktop installation is an important step to ensure a smooth and successful virtualization experience. Before you begin the installation process, it's essential to review your Mac's hardware specifications to ensure that it meets the system requirements for Parallels Desktop. You can find the detailed system requirements on the official Parallels website, including information about supported Mac models, macOS versions, and minimum hardware specifications. Upgrading your Mac's hardware, such as adding more RAM or upgrading your hard drive to an SSD, can significantly improve the performance of virtual machines within Parallels Desktop. Before proceeding, it's also advisable to back up your important data on your Mac. While the installation of Parallels Desktop itself is unlikely to cause data loss, accidents can happen, and it's better to be safe than sorry. You can use Time Machine or any other reliable backup solution to create a backup of your Mac's data. Next, you'll want to ensure that your Mac's operating system is up to date. Having the latest macOS updates and security patches is essential for a stable and secure virtualization experience. Check for available updates by going to the Apple menu, selecting "About This Mac," and clicking on "Software Update." If updates are available, follow the on-screen instructions to install them. Parallels Desktop typically supports the latest macOS versions, so it's a good idea to keep your Mac's operating system current. Before installing Parallels Desktop, you should also review your software applications and ensure that they are compatible with virtualization. Some software, especially security or system-related applications, may conflict with virtualization software. Visit the websites of your critical applications or consult their documentation to check for any known compatibility issues with virtualization software like Parallels Desktop. In some cases, you may need to adjust settings or configurations within these applications to work correctly within virtual machines. Additionally, it's advisable to close any open applications and save your work before beginning the installation process. While Parallels Desktop installation is generally straightforward and shouldn't disrupt your existing applications, it's a good practice to have a clean slate and minimize potential issues during installation. Before proceeding, ensure that you have a valid license or activation key for Parallels Desktop. You'll need this key during the installation process to activate the software. If you don't have a license yet, you can purchase one from the Parallels website or an authorized reseller. During the installation process, Parallels Desktop will prompt you to enter your license key to activate the software. Additionally, make sure you have a stable and reliable internet connection before starting the installation. A strong internet connection is essential for downloading and installing Parallels Desktop and its updates. If your internet connection is slow or unreliable, it may result in a longer installation process and potential interruptions. Now, let's discuss the installation process itself. To install Parallels Desktop on your Mac, you'll need to download the installation package from the official Parallels website. Visit the Parallels website and locate the Parallels Desktop product page. There, you'll find an option to download the latest version of Parallels Desktop. Click on the download link, and the installation package will begin downloading to your Mac. Once the download is complete, locate the downloaded installation package in your Downloads folder or the location you specified. Double-click on the installation package to begin the installation process. You'll be guided through a series of on-screen instructions to install Parallels Desktop. Follow these instructions carefully, and be prepared to enter your license key when prompted. During the installation, Parallels Desktop will also request permission to install additional components, such as system extensions. Grant the necessary permissions for a successful installation. After the installation is complete, you can launch Parallels Desktop from your Applications folder. Upon launching Parallels Desktop for the first time, you'll need to activate the software using your license key. Enter the key when prompted, and the software will validate and activate your license. Once activated, you can start creating and configuring virtual machines to run different operating systems on your Mac. Remember that Parallels Desktop allows you to run Windows, Linux, and various other operating systems alongside macOS. It provides a user-friendly interface for managing virtual machines, adjusting settings, and installing guest operating systems. Additionally, you can use Parallels Desktop's features like Coherence mode, snapshots, and shared folders to enhance your virtualization experience. In summary, preparing your Mac for Parallels Desktop installation involves reviewing system requirements, backing up data, updating your Mac's operating system, checking application compatibility, and ensuring a reliable internet connection. Once your Mac is ready, downloading and installing Parallels Desktop is a straightforward process that involves entering your license key and following on-screen instructions. After installation and activation, you can begin creating virtual machines and exploring the world of virtualization on your Mac.

Chapter 3: Creating and Configuring Virtual Machines

Installing and configuring guest tools is an essential step in optimizing the performance and functionality of virtual machines (VMs) within Parallels Desktop. Guest tools, often referred to as guest additions or guest extensions, are sets of software utilities and drivers designed to enhance the integration between the host system (macOS) and the guest operating system running within the VM. In the context of Parallels Desktop, guest tools are specific to each guest operating system, whether it's Windows, Linux, or another supported OS. The installation process for guest tools varies depending on the guest OS, so it's essential to follow the instructions tailored to your VM's operating system. In this chapter, we will explore the general concepts and benefits of installing and configuring guest tools in a Parallels Desktop VM. The primary purpose of guest tools is to bridge the gap between the host and guest operating systems, providing a seamless and integrated user experience. One of the key benefits of installing guest tools is improved display and graphics performance. By installing the appropriate graphics drivers and utilities, you can achieve higher screen resolutions, smoother graphics rendering, and support for features like hardware-accelerated 3D graphics. This is particularly important when running operating systems that require robust graphics capabilities, such as Windows for gaming or graphic design applications. Another critical aspect of guest tools is enhancing mouse and keyboard integration. Without guest tools, the mouse cursor may be trapped inside the VM window, requiring you to press a key to release it. Guest tools resolve this issue, allowing you to move the cursor seamlessly between the host and guest OS environments. Additionally, guest tools enable features like automatic mouse capture when you move the mouse inside the VM window, simplifying the interaction between the two systems. Clipboard sharing is another significant advantage of installing guest tools. With guest tools in place, you can easily copy and paste text and files between the host macOS and the guest OS within the VM. This feature streamlines workflows and eliminates the need for manual file transfers, making it much more convenient to work with data between the two environments. File sharing and drag-and-drop functionality are extended with guest tools. You can share folders between the host and guest OS, allowing for seamless file access and transfer. By simply dragging and dropping files between the macOS desktop and the VM window, you can effortlessly move data back and forth. This is especially useful for tasks like editing documents or accessing files stored on your Mac while working within the VM. Shared folders also simplify the process of transferring files to and from the VM, eliminating the need for email attachments or external storage devices. Printing from a VM is greatly improved with the installation of guest tools. Guest tools provide printer drivers and integration with the macOS printing system, allowing you to print documents directly from the VM to your Mac's connected printers. This eliminates the need to transfer files to the host OS for printing and ensures that you can easily produce hard copies of documents from within the VM. Sound support is another advantage of guest tools. By installing the appropriate audio drivers and utilities, you can enable sound playback and recording within the VM. This is important for tasks that involve multimedia content, such as watching videos, participating in virtual meetings, or using audio editing software within the VM. Guest tools also enhance the performance of storage devices within the VM. With optimized storage drivers, you can achieve better read and write speeds for virtual hard disks and other storage devices attached to the VM. This is particularly beneficial when working with large files or data-intensive applications. Furthermore, guest tools provide features like automatic adjustment of the guest OS resolution to fit the VM window. This ensures that the guest OS display adapts to the size of the VM window, improving usability and reducing the need for manual adjustments. Guest tools may also offer additional utilities and features specific to the guest OS. For example, in Windows VMs, guest tools often include utilities for seamless mode, which allows you to run Windows applications alongside macOS applications in a unified desktop experience similar to Parallels Desktop's Coherence mode. Installing and configuring guest tools is typically straightforward and involves a few simple steps. Once you've created a virtual machine and installed the guest operating system, you can mount the guest tools ISO or installer file. This file is typically included with your virtualization software or can be downloaded from the official website. After mounting the ISO or running the installer, you'll follow the on-screen instructions to install the guest tools within the VM. The installation process may require you to reboot the guest OS to complete the installation. Once guest tools are installed, you can configure their settings to tailor the integration and functionality to your preferences. These settings may include enabling or disabling features like clipboard sharing, drag-and-drop, and folder sharing. You can access these settings through the guest tools control panel or settings menu within the guest OS. It's essential to keep guest tools up to date by periodically checking for updates and applying them to ensure compatibility with your virtualization software and host OS. In summary, installing and configuring guest tools is a crucial step in optimizing the performance and usability of virtual machines within Parallels Desktop. These tools bridge the gap between the host and guest operating systems, providing benefits such as enhanced display and graphics performance, seamless mouse and keyboard integration, clipboard sharing, file sharing, improved printing support, sound playback and recording, and optimized storage performance. By following the specific installation instructions for your guest OS and configuring guest tool settings to your preferences, you can enjoy a seamless and integrated virtualization experience on your Mac.

Chapter 4: Seamless Integration with Mac OS

Customizing and managing virtual machines (VMs) is a fundamental aspect of virtualization that allows users to tailor their VMs to specific requirements and maintain their optimal performance. In Parallels Desktop, you have a wide range of options and tools at your disposal to customize and manage your VMs effectively. One of the first steps in customizing a VM is configuring its hardware settings to match your needs. You can adjust the number of CPU cores and allocate specific amounts of memory (RAM) to each VM based on the workload it will handle. Customizing hardware resources ensures that VMs have the necessary computational power and memory capacity to run applications smoothly. For example, a VM running resource-intensive tasks like 3D rendering may require more CPU cores and RAM than a VM used for general office work. Parallels Desktop allows you to add or remove virtual hardware components, such as hard disks and network adapters, as needed. This flexibility enables you to expand storage capacity or fine-tune network configurations to meet your VM's requirements. Virtual hard disks can be resized, and additional hard disks can be attached to accommodate growing data storage needs. Managing snapshots is another essential aspect of VM customization and management. Snapshots capture the state of a VM at a specific point in time, allowing you to revert to that state if needed. Before making significant changes or updates to a VM, it's a good practice to create a snapshot. This way, you can easily roll back to the previous state if any issues arise during the customization process. Parallels Desktop provides tools for taking, managing, and deleting snapshots, ensuring that you can maintain the desired VM state at any given moment. While customizing VMs, it's essential to consider the guest operating system's settings and configurations. Each guest OS may have specific settings related to display resolution, power management, and network configuration. For example, in a Windows VM, you can adjust the screen resolution, enable or disable features like Aero Glass, and configure power-saving settings. In Linux VMs, you can customize desktop environments, network settings, and system preferences. These guest OS settings allow you to tailor the VM environment to your preferences and requirements. Parallels Desktop provides integration features that enhance the usability of VMs. One of these features is Coherence mode, which allows you to run Windows applications seamlessly alongside macOS applications. In Coherence mode, Windows applications appear as if they are running natively on the macOS desktop, eliminating the need to switch between different VM windows. This feature enhances productivity by creating a unified computing experience. Another integration feature is the ability to share folders and drag-and-drop files between the host macOS and VMs. This simplifies the process of transferring files and data, making it more convenient to work between the two environments. Clipboard sharing is yet another integration feature that allows you to copy and paste text and files between macOS and VMs, further streamlining workflows. Parallels Desktop also supports the use of USB devices within VMs, enabling you to connect and use USB peripherals, such as external hard drives, printers, and smartphones. This ensures that you can work with your preferred hardware while using virtual machines. To manage multiple VMs efficiently, Parallels Desktop provides features for organizing and grouping VMs. You can create folders and categories to categorize VMs based on their purpose, department, or project. This organizational structure simplifies VM management, especially when you have several VMs for various tasks. Additionally, you can customize the appearance of VM icons and assign different colors to VMs for easy identification. Parallels Desktop offers options for adjusting the interaction between the host macOS and VMs. You can configure settings related to mouse and keyboard behavior, ensuring that the cursor movement and keypresses work as expected within VMs. For instance, you can choose whether the mouse cursor should be confined to the VM window or freely move between the host and guest OS. Keyboard shortcuts and input methods can also be customized to match your preferences. Performance optimization is a vital aspect of VM management. Parallels Desktop provides tools for monitoring and fine-tuning VM performance. You can view real-time performance metrics, such as CPU and memory usage, within the Parallels Desktop Control Center. This information helps you identify potential performance bottlenecks and adjust VM settings accordingly. To optimize disk space usage, you can clean up virtual hard disks by removing unnecessary files and reclaiming unused space. Parallels Desktop also offers features for adjusting the display and graphics settings of VMs. You can customize display resolutions, enable or disable hardware acceleration, and adjust 3D graphics settings to match the requirements of specific applications or tasks. By tailoring these settings, you can ensure a smooth and visually pleasing experience within VMs. Another aspect of VM customization is managing software and applications within the VM environment. You can install, update, and remove software as needed, just as you would on a physical computer. It's essential to keep the guest OS and installed applications up to date with the latest security patches and updates. Regular software maintenance ensures the security and stability of VMs. Finally, backup and recovery strategies are crucial components of VM management. Parallels Desktop allows you to create and manage snapshots, which serve as backups that can be used to restore a VM to a previous state. In addition to snapshots, you should consider implementing backup solutions within the guest OS to safeguard important data. Overall, customizing and managing virtual machines in Parallels Desktop involves configuring hardware settings, managing snapshots, adjusting guest OS settings, and leveraging integration features to enhance usability. Efficient VM organization, performance optimization, software management, and backup strategies contribute to a well-maintained and productive virtualization environment. By understanding and utilizing the customization and management tools available in Parallels Desktop, you can make the most of your virtual machines and achieve your desired computing experience.

Chapter 5: Advanced Storage Management

Using Coherence mode in virtualization software, such as Parallels Desktop, offers a seamless integration experience between your host operating system, like macOS, and the guest operating system running within a virtual machine. Coherence mode aims to create a unified desktop environment where you can run applications from the guest OS alongside those from your host OS, as if they are all part of a single computing environment. This integration enhances productivity by eliminating the need to switch between different virtual machine windows or environments. When you enable Coherence mode, your virtual machine's desktop and applications become seamlessly integrated into your macOS desktop. The result is a more efficient workflow, as you can access and use both macOS and guest OS applications from a single desktop. One of the key features of Coherence mode is the ability to run Windows applications alongside macOS applications. For example, you can open a Windows application like Microsoft Word directly from your macOS desktop, and it will appear as if it's running natively on your Mac. The Windows application window behaves just like any other macOS application window, complete with its own icon in the macOS Dock. This eliminates the need to navigate through your virtual machine's Windows desktop or Start menu to launch applications. To access Coherence mode in Parallels Desktop, you typically click on a specific button or menu option within the virtual machine window. Once Coherence mode is activated, your virtual machine's desktop background disappears, and the Windows or guest OS applications integrate seamlessly with your macOS desktop. You can easily switch between macOS and guest OS applications without any visual distinction, creating a more fluid and user-friendly experience. Additionally, Coherence mode allows you to interact with guest OS applications using familiar macOS conventions. For instance, you can use macOS keyboard shortcuts, like Command+C for copy and Command+V for paste, within Windows applications. This consistent experience reduces the learning curve and enhances your overall efficiency when working with applications from different operating systems. Coherence mode also offers convenience when it comes to file management. You can drag and drop files between macOS and guest OS applications effortlessly, making it easy to transfer data between the two environments. Copying text or images from a macOS application and pasting them into a Windows application (or vice versa) is just as straightforward as within a single operating system. Clipboard sharing is seamless in Coherence mode, further enhancing your workflow. It's important to note that Coherence mode is not limited to Windows applications; it works with applications from various guest operating systems, such as Linux or other Windows versions. This flexibility allows you to choose the best tool or application for your tasks, regardless of the operating system it runs on. Another aspect of

Coherence mode is the ability to customize the appearance and behavior of virtual machine applications within the macOS environment. You can adjust the size of Windows application windows, resize them, and position them on your macOS desktop according to your preferences. This customization ensures that your integrated workspace is tailored to your needs. Coherence mode also offers options for managing virtual machine windows and controlling their behavior. For instance, you can minimize, maximize, or close virtual machine windows just like you would with macOS applications. Virtual machine windows can also be grouped or tabbed together on the macOS Dock for easy access and organization. Coherence mode is designed to provide a smooth and intuitive integration experience, allowing you to focus on your work without being distracted by the complexities of managing multiple operating systems. However, it's important to keep in mind that Coherence mode requires a certain level of system resources, including CPU and memory, to operate smoothly. Ensure that your Mac meets the system requirements for virtualization and allocate adequate resources to your virtual machine for the best Coherence mode experience. Additionally, some applications may perform differently in Coherence mode compared to running them directly within their respective operating systems. It's a good practice to test applications in Coherence mode to ensure that they function as expected. In summary, using Coherence mode in virtualization software like Parallels Desktop offers a seamless integration experience between your host and guest operating systems. Coherence mode allows you to run applications from different operating systems, such as Windows or Linux, alongside your macOS applications on a unified desktop. This integration enhances productivity, as you can work with multiple applications without switching between different virtual machine windows or environments. Coherence mode also provides convenience for tasks like file management, clipboard sharing, and customization of the integrated workspace. By leveraging the capabilities of Coherence mode, you can create a more efficient and user-friendly computing experience on your Mac.

Chapter 6: Snapshot Strategies and Cloning Techniques

Advanced disk management in Parallels Desktop is a crucial aspect of optimizing the performance and efficiency of your virtual machines (VMs). As you work with VMs, you may encounter scenarios where you need to manage virtual hard disks, allocate storage resources, and ensure data integrity. Parallels Desktop provides a range of tools and features to help you manage disks effectively. One of the primary tasks in advanced disk management is resizing virtual hard disks. Over time, your VM's storage needs may change, and you might need to increase or decrease the size of its virtual hard disk. Parallels Desktop allows you to resize virtual hard disks easily, ensuring that your VM has adequate storage space. You can increase the size of a virtual hard disk to accommodate growing data or applications, or you can reduce its size to free up space on your Mac's physical storage. When resizing a virtual hard disk, it's important to remember that you can only increase its size if there is unallocated space within the virtual machine's file system. If you need to decrease the size of a virtual hard disk, you should first shrink the file system and remove any unnecessary data from within the VM to ensure a successful resizing process. Another essential aspect of advanced disk management is adding and removing virtual hard disks from your VM. Parallels Desktop allows you to attach additional virtual hard disks to a VM to expand its storage capacity. You can create new virtual hard disks or attach existing ones to meet your specific storage requirements. This flexibility is particularly useful when you need to separate data storage, create backup disks, or allocate different types of storage for your VMs. Conversely, you can also remove virtual hard disks that are no longer needed to free up resources. Parallels Desktop makes it straightforward to attach or detach virtual hard disks as part of your disk management strategy. Effective disk management also includes optimizing storage performance within your VMs. Parallels Desktop supports a range of virtual hard disk formats, including standard and optimized formats. Optimized formats provide better performance by reducing disk I/O and improving read and write operations. When creating new virtual hard disks or converting existing ones, choosing an optimized format can significantly enhance the overall performance of your VMs. Another important aspect of disk management is monitoring and maintaining the health of virtual hard disks. Parallels Desktop offers disk utility tools that allow you to check the integrity of your virtual hard disks and repair any issues that may arise. Disk utilities help ensure that your VMs remain reliable and free from data corruption. Regular disk maintenance can prevent potential problems and ensure the smooth operation of your VMs. Additionally, as part of advanced disk management, you should consider implementing backup and recovery strategies. Regularly creating snapshots or backups of your VMs and their associated virtual hard disks is essential for data protection. Parallels Desktop provides tools to create and manage snapshots, allowing you to capture the state of your VMs at specific points in time. These snapshots can be used for backup and recovery purposes, enabling you to restore your VMs to a previous state if needed. It's essential to establish a backup schedule and keep snapshots up to date to safeguard your data. When managing virtual hard disks, it's also crucial to consider the file system and partitioning within your VMs. Parallels Desktop supports a variety of guest operating systems, each with its own file system and partitioning requirements. You should familiarize yourself with the file systems used by your guest OS and understand how to create and manage partitions within the VM. This knowledge is particularly valuable when you need to allocate storage resources efficiently or manage data storage within your VMs. Furthermore, advanced disk management includes optimizing the performance of virtual hard disks. Parallels Desktop offers features to improve disk performance, such as enabling write-caching and using SSD optimization for virtual hard disks. These optimizations can lead to faster disk access and improved overall VM performance. However, it's essential to balance performance optimizations with data integrity and ensure that your VMs remain stable. To maintain an efficient and organized disk management strategy, you can create a plan for allocating storage resources among your VMs. Consider the specific requirements of each VM, such as storage capacity, disk format, and performance needs. By planning ahead and allocating resources accordingly, you can avoid storage-related performance bottlenecks and ensure that your VMs run smoothly. In summary, advanced disk management in Parallels Desktop is a critical aspect of optimizing the performance and efficiency of your virtual machines. Effective disk management includes resizing virtual hard disks, adding or removing virtual hard disks, optimizing storage performance, monitoring disk health, implementing backup and recovery strategies, and understanding file systems and partitioning within your VMs. By mastering these aspects of disk management, you can ensure the reliability and performance of your VMs while efficiently managing storage resources.

Chapter 7: Performance Tuning and Optimization

Working with snapshots in Parallels Desktop is an essential part of managing and safeguarding your virtual machines (VMs). Snapshots are a powerful feature that allows you to capture the current state of a VM at a specific point in time. These snapshots serve as a backup of your VM's configuration and data, providing you with a safety net in case anything goes wrong during software updates, configuration changes, or other operations. When you create a snapshot, Parallels Desktop records the current state of your VM, including its virtual hard disk, memory contents, and virtual machine settings. This snapshot becomes a point of reference that you can return to if you encounter issues or need to restore your VM to a previous state. Snapshots are particularly valuable when you're about to perform significant changes to your VM, such as installing new software, configuring system settings, or testing updates. Before making these changes, it's a best practice to create a snapshot to ensure that you can revert to a stable state if anything goes awry. To create a snapshot in Parallels Desktop, you can typically use the snapshot feature within the virtual machine management interface. You'll be prompted to give the snapshot a descriptive name and, optionally, add a brief description to help you remember its purpose or context. This naming convention makes it easier to identify and manage snapshots, especially when you have multiple snapshots for a single VM. Once the snapshot is created, you can continue with your planned changes or updates within the VM. Parallels Desktop allows you to create multiple snapshots for a VM, enabling you to capture different states of the VM over time. For example, you might create snapshots before and after installing software updates, creating a baseline snapshot for your VM, and creating snapshots for different project milestones. These snapshots give you the flexibility to restore your VM to various points in its history, depending on your needs. Managing and using snapshots effectively involves several key considerations. One important factor is snapshot naming and organization. As mentioned earlier, giving each snapshot a meaningful name and description helps you keep track of their purposes. You can also categorize snapshots based on their context, such as "Before Updates" or "Project A Milestone." This organization makes it easier to navigate and manage snapshots when you have multiple VMs and snapshots to handle. In addition to naming and categorizing snapshots, you should establish a snapshot management routine. This routine includes regular maintenance tasks like periodically deleting older snapshots that are no longer needed. While snapshots are valuable for recovery and testing purposes, they can consume significant disk space over time. Deleting unnecessary snapshots helps free up storage resources and keeps your VMs running efficiently. However, when deleting snapshots, it's essential to consider the dependencies between snapshots. In Parallels Desktop, snapshots are organized in a chain, with each snapshot building upon the previous one. Deleting an intermediate snapshot in the chain can impact the integrity of subsequent snapshots. To avoid issues, it's advisable to delete snapshots from the oldest to the newest in the chain. Another aspect of snapshot management is restoring a VM to a previous snapshot. When you encounter problems or need to roll back to a specific point in time, you can use Parallels Desktop to restore your VM to the state captured in a snapshot. This process essentially reverts the VM to the configuration and data saved in the selected snapshot. It's important to note that when you restore a snapshot, any changes made to the VM after that snapshot was created will be lost. For example, if you created a snapshot before installing a new application and later installed additional software and made configuration changes, restoring to the snapshot would remove all those post-snapshot modifications. Therefore, it's crucial to carefully consider which snapshot to restore to and to back up any critical data or changes before performing a snapshot restoration. In addition to traditional snapshots, Parallels Desktop offers an interesting feature called "Snapshots with Checkpoints." This feature allows you to create snapshots that preserve the current state of your VM but continue to allow the VM to run and be modified. Snapshots with Checkpoints are useful when you want to save the current state of a VM for future reference but also want to keep using the VM without interruption. These snapshots capture the VM's state at a specific moment while allowing you to continue working, making them a versatile tool for managing VMs. Furthermore, Parallels Desktop offers a feature called "Scheduled Snapshots," which automates the snapshot creation process. You can set up scheduled snapshots to capture the state of your VM at specific intervals, such as daily or weekly. This automated approach ensures that you have regular backups of your VMs without manual intervention. Scheduled snapshots are particularly helpful for maintaining data consistency and minimizing the risk of data loss. While snapshots are a valuable tool for managing VMs, they are not a substitute for regular backups of your VMs and their data. Snapshots primarily capture the state of a VM's virtual hard disk and memory contents but do not address external data, such as files and documents stored within the VM. To ensure comprehensive data protection, it's essential to implement a backup strategy that includes both snapshots and regular backups of your VMs. In summary, working with snapshots in Parallels Desktop is an essential part of managing and safeguarding your virtual machines. Snapshots allow you to capture the current state of your VMs, providing a safety net for software updates, configuration changes, and testing. Effective snapshot management involves naming and organizing snapshots, establishing a routine for snapshot maintenance, and understanding the implications of snapshot restoration. Additionally, features like Snapshots with Checkpoints and Scheduled Snapshots offer versatility and automation in managing snapshots. While snapshots are a valuable tool for VM management, they should be complemented by regular backups to ensure comprehensive data protection.

Chapter 8: Networking Strategies for Parallels Desktop

Performance optimization in Parallels Desktop is crucial for ensuring that your virtual machines (VMs) run smoothly and efficiently on your Mac. Optimizing the performance of your VMs enhances productivity and provides a seamless user experience. Parallels Desktop offers a range of strategies and features to help you achieve optimal VM performance. One of the key factors in performance optimization is resource allocation. When you create a virtual machine, you can specify how many CPU cores, how much memory (RAM), and how much storage space it should use. It's essential to allocate resources based on the specific requirements of the VM and the tasks it will perform. Adequate CPU and RAM allocation ensures that the VM has enough computing power to run applications and tasks smoothly. However, it's also important not to over-allocate resources, as this can lead to resource contention and decreased performance for both the VM and your host system. Balancing resource allocation is a critical aspect of performance optimization. Parallels Desktop provides tools to adjust resource allocation even after a VM is created, allowing you to fine-tune the VM's performance as needed. Another performance optimization strategy is selecting the right virtual hard disk format. Parallels Desktop supports various disk formats, including standard and optimized formats. Optimized formats are designed for improved performance and efficiency. By choosing an optimized format for your virtual hard disks, you can enhance read and write operations, resulting in faster disk access within your VMs. This optimization is particularly beneficial for tasks that involve significant disk I/O, such as database operations and file transfers. Additionally, enabling write-caching for virtual hard disks can further boost performance by allowing data to be temporarily stored in memory before being written to disk. Write-caching reduces disk I/O, resulting in quicker response times for applications and tasks. However, it's important to use write-caching cautiously, as it may increase the risk of data loss in the event of a system crash or power failure. To maintain data integrity, you should ensure that your VMs are regularly backed up. In addition to resource allocation and disk format optimization, Parallels Desktop offers features to improve graphics performance. For tasks that require intensive graphics processing, such as video editing or 3D rendering, you can enable 3D acceleration for your VMs. This feature leverages the capabilities of your Mac's graphics hardware to enhance the rendering of 3D graphics within the VM. Enabling 3D acceleration can significantly improve the performance of graphics-intensive applications running in your VMs. However, not all VMs and guest operating systems support 3D acceleration, so it's essential to check compatibility before enabling this feature. Another performance optimization strategy is using SSD (Solid State Drive) optimization for virtual hard disks. If your Mac is equipped with an SSD, Parallels Desktop allows you to optimize your VMs for SSD storage. This optimization leverages the high-speed read and write capabilities of SSDs to enhance overall VM performance. Using an SSD-optimized virtual hard disk format and enabling SSD optimization can lead to faster boot times, application launches, and file access within your VMs. It's important to note that the benefits of SSD optimization are most pronounced when both your host system and VMs are stored on SSDs. In addition to these hardware-related strategies, Parallels Desktop offers features to improve the overall responsiveness of your VMs. For example, you can enable Coherence mode, which seamlessly integrates your VMs' applications with your Mac's desktop environment. This integration allows you to run Windows applications alongside macOS applications as if they are all part of a single computing environment. Coherence mode enhances workflow efficiency by eliminating the need to switch between virtual machine windows. Furthermore, Parallels Desktop allows you to allocate more CPU cores to specific virtual machines that require additional processing power. By adjusting CPU core allocation, you can ensure that resource-intensive applications within a VM perform optimally without affecting the performance of other VMs or your host system. When it comes to network performance optimization, Parallels Desktop provides features to configure virtual networks efficiently. You can set up bridged networking to allow your VMs to access the network directly through your Mac's network adapter. Bridged networking offers the best network performance, as it provides VMs with their own IP addresses on the local network. This configuration is ideal for tasks that require high network bandwidth, such as web development or network testing. Another network optimization strategy is using shared networking for VMs that do not require direct access to the local network. Shared networking allows VMs to share your Mac's network connection, providing internet access while conserving network resources. Additionally, Parallels Desktop offers the ability to configure port forwarding, enabling specific network services or applications within a VM to be accessible from external devices or the host system. This feature is useful for scenarios where you need to host web servers, run remote desktop services, or test network applications within your VMs. To further enhance performance, it's essential to keep your virtualization software and guest operating systems up to date with the latest updates, patches, and drivers. Regularly checking for software updates and applying them ensures that you have access to performance improvements and bug fixes. Additionally, optimizing your VMs for specific use cases can lead to significant performance gains. For example, if you plan to use a VM primarily for gaming, configuring the VM's settings to prioritize graphics and input devices can result in a better gaming experience. On the other hand, if you intend to use a VM for software development, allocating additional CPU and memory resources can improve compile times and responsiveness. In summary, performance optimization in Parallels Desktop is essential for achieving efficient and responsive virtual machine operations. Optimizing resource allocation, selecting the right virtual hard disk format, enabling 3D acceleration, and leveraging SSD optimization are crucial strategies to enhance performance. Additionally, using features like Coherence mode, adjusting CPU core allocation, and configuring network settings contribute to a smoother user experience. Regularly updating virtualization software and guest operating systems, as well as optimizing VMs for specific use cases, further contribute to performance improvements. By implementing these strategies and features, you can ensure that your VMs run at their best, whether you're running applications, developing software, or performing other tasks within your virtualized environment.

Chapter 9: Backup and Recovery Strategies

Configuring networking options in Parallels Desktop is a critical aspect of creating a functional and connected virtual environment. Effective network configuration allows your virtual machines (VMs) to communicate with each other, access the internet, and interact with devices on your local network. Parallels Desktop provides various networking options and features to tailor your VMs' network connectivity to your specific needs. One of the fundamental networking options is the choice of network mode for your VMs. Parallels Desktop offers several network modes, each with its own characteristics and use cases. The default mode is often set to "Shared" networking, which allows your VMs to share your Mac's network connection, typically through Network Address Translation (NAT). This mode is suitable for most scenarios, providing internet access to your VMs while keeping them isolated from your local network. However, you may need to configure other network modes for specific purposes. For instance, "Bridged" networking mode allows your VMs to have their own IP addresses on your local network, making them directly accessible to other devices on the network. This mode is ideal for scenarios where you want your VMs to function as separate entities on your network, such as running web servers or accessing networked resources. Another network mode, "Host-Only" networking, creates a private network that includes your Mac and all VMs using host-only mode.

This mode is useful for creating isolated network environments for testing or development purposes. Additionally, Parallels Desktop provides the option to set up custom network configurations to suit your specific requirements. Custom network configurations allow you to define IP address ranges, subnet masks, and other networking parameters to create a tailored network environment for your VMs. Network configuration also includes the ability to configure port forwarding. Port forwarding allows you to redirect network traffic from specific ports on your Mac to corresponding ports on a VM. This feature is valuable for scenarios where you need to expose specific network services within a VM to the external network or access services running within your VM from your Mac. For example, you can use port forwarding to make a web server running in a VM accessible from your Mac's web browser. In addition to network modes and port forwarding, Parallels Desktop provides features to enhance network performance and functionality. One such feature is the "Shared Profile" option, which allows VMs to share their networking settings with each other. This means that if you have multiple VMs, you can configure one VM with the desired network settings and then share those settings with other VMs. This feature simplifies the process of configuring network settings for multiple VMs with similar requirements. Furthermore, Parallels Desktop allows you to configure the network adapter type for your VMs. The choice of network adapter type can impact network performance and compatibility with specific guest operating systems.

Parallels Desktop offers various network adapter types, including Intel PRO/1000, Realtek RTL8029, and Parallels' own network adapter. Selecting the appropriate network adapter type ensures compatibility and optimal network performance for your VMs. To streamline network configuration, Parallels Desktop provides a network settings editor that allows you to manage and modify your VMs' network settings easily. This editor provides a user-friendly interface for configuring network modes, custom network parameters, and port forwarding rules. By using the network settings editor, you can quickly adapt your VMs' network configuration to meet changing requirements. When configuring network options, it's essential to consider security. Parallels Desktop provides built-in security features to protect your VMs and network connections. For example, you can enable the firewall feature to filter incoming and outgoing network traffic for your VMs. Firewall rules can be defined to allow or block specific network services or applications within your VMs. This granular control over network traffic helps enhance security and prevent unauthorized access. Additionally, Parallels Desktop offers the option to create network profiles, allowing you to save and switch between different network configurations. Network profiles are particularly useful when you frequently switch between various network environments, such as home, office, or public Wi-Fi networks. By creating and saving network profiles, you can quickly adapt your VMs' network settings to match your current network environment. When configuring networking options, it's important to consider the overall network architecture and how your VMs will interact with other devices and services on the network. For example, if you plan to set up a web server in a VM for development purposes, you need to ensure that port forwarding is correctly configured to allow external access to the web server. On the other hand, if you're using VMs for testing and want to create an isolated network environment, you may opt for host-only networking to ensure network separation. Network configuration also plays a crucial role in scenarios where you need to test networked applications or simulate complex network architectures. For these situations, Parallels Desktop's flexibility in configuring network options allows you to create tailored network environments that mimic real-world scenarios. In summary, configuring networking options in Parallels Desktop is a fundamental aspect of creating a functional and connected virtual environment. Choosing the appropriate network mode, configuring port forwarding, setting up custom network configurations, and utilizing features like shared profiles and network settings editors allow you to fine-tune network connectivity for your VMs. Considering security measures, such as enabling firewalls and creating network profiles, ensures that your VMs are protected while interacting with external networks. By carefully configuring networking options and adapting them to your specific needs, you can create a seamless and secure network environment for your virtual machines.

Chapter 10: Advanced Troubleshooting and Maintenance

Backup and recovery are essential aspects of maintaining data integrity and continuity in your virtualized environment using Parallels Desktop. Effective backup and recovery practices ensure that you can recover your virtual machines (VMs) and data in case of unexpected events, such as hardware failures or data corruption. Parallels Desktop offers several backup and recovery options to safeguard your VMs and streamline the restoration process. One of the best practices for backup and recovery in Parallels Desktop is to establish a regular backup schedule. Creating a backup schedule ensures that your VMs are consistently backed up at predefined intervals, reducing the risk of data loss. Regular backups provide you with multiple restore points, allowing you to recover VMs to a specific state based on your needs. When configuring your backup schedule, consider factors such as the frequency of data changes within your VMs and the importance of the data. Critical VMs with frequently changing data may require more frequent backups, while less critical VMs can be backed up less frequently. Parallels Desktop offers a user-friendly backup feature that allows you to automate the backup process. You can set up backup plans that specify which VMs to back up, the backup destination, and the backup frequency. Automated backups simplify the backup process, ensuring that your

VMs are consistently protected without manual intervention. Additionally, Parallels Desktop allows you to choose between incremental and full backups. Incremental backups capture only the changes made since the last backup, conserving storage space and reducing backup time. Full backups, on the other hand, capture the entire VM, providing a complete snapshot of the VM's state. A combination of both incremental and periodic full backups can provide a balanced approach to data protection. Another best practice for backup and recovery in Parallels Desktop is to store backups in separate locations or on external storage devices. Storing backups in a location separate from the source VMs helps safeguard against data loss due to events like hardware failures, theft, or disasters. You can configure Parallels Desktop to save backups to external hard drives, network-attached storage (NAS) devices, or cloud storage services for added redundancy. Cloud storage services offer the advantage of off-site backup, ensuring that your data remains accessible even if your physical location is compromised. When selecting an external storage location or cloud storage provider, consider factors such as data security, accessibility, and cost. Encryption plays a crucial role in securing your backup data. Parallels Desktop provides the option to encrypt backups, adding an additional layer of protection to your VM data. Encryption ensures that even if backup files fall into the wrong hands, they remain unreadable without the encryption key. By enabling backup encryption, you can safeguard sensitive data and comply with data protection regulations. Furthermore, it's important to test your backup and recovery process periodically to ensure that it functions as expected. Testing backups involves verifying that you can successfully restore VMs from backup files and that the restored VMs function correctly. Regular testing helps identify any issues with the backup and recovery process and allows you to address them proactively. In addition to testing, documenting your backup and recovery procedures is a crucial best practice. Documentation provides a reference for your backup strategy, ensuring that you and your team can follow established procedures in case of a data loss event. Include details such as the backup schedule, backup destination, encryption settings, and steps for restoring VMs. By maintaining comprehensive documentation, you reduce the risk of errors and delays during the recovery process. Another consideration in backup and recovery is versioning. Parallels Desktop allows you to create multiple versions of your VMs, which can serve as additional restore points. Versioning is particularly useful when you need to recover data or configurations from a specific point in time. By preserving multiple versions of your VMs, you have greater flexibility in selecting a restore point that aligns with your recovery objectives. In case of critical data loss, you can restore an earlier version of your VM to minimize the impact of data corruption or accidental deletion. Parallels Desktop also offers the option to enable snapshots, which are similar to point-in-time backups. Snapshots capture the current state of a VM, allowing you to revert to that state at any time. This feature is useful when you want to experiment with software configurations or test updates without affecting your VM's stability. However, it's important to manage snapshots carefully to prevent excessive disk usage. Regularly review and delete unnecessary snapshots to optimize storage utilization. When it comes to the recovery process, Parallels Desktop provides straightforward methods for restoring VMs. You can initiate the restoration from within the Parallels Desktop interface, selecting the desired backup and specifying the destination. The restoration process involves copying the backup files to the destination location and configuring the VM to use the restored data. Once the restoration is complete, you can start the VM, and it will run based on the restored state. In case of catastrophic hardware failure or data corruption, you may need to recreate your virtual environment from backups. In such scenarios, having a well-documented disaster recovery plan is essential. Your disaster recovery plan should outline the steps to rebuild your virtual environment, including installing Parallels Desktop, restoring VMs from backups, and configuring network settings. By following a predefined plan, you can minimize downtime and expedite the recovery process. Lastly, monitoring the health and status of your backups is a critical best practice. Parallels Desktop offers tools and notifications to inform you of backup completion, errors, or warnings. Regularly review backup logs and notifications to ensure that backups are occurring as scheduled and that no issues require attention. Monitoring ensures that your backup strategy remains effective and that you can address any backup-related issues promptly. In summary, backup and recovery best practices in Parallels Desktop are essential for safeguarding your virtual machines and data. Establishing a regular backup schedule, automating backups, and storing backups in separate locations or on external storage devices help protect against data loss. Encryption, testing, and documentation enhance the security and reliability of your backup strategy. Versioning and snapshots provide flexibility and options for data recovery. Having a disaster recovery plan in place ensures a systematic approach to restoring your virtual environment in case of catastrophic events. Monitoring and regular review of backup logs help maintain the integrity of your backup process. By implementing these best practices, you can confidently manage backup and recovery in your Parallels Desktop virtualized environment, ensuring data availability and business continuity.

BOOK 4
CITRIX HYPERVISOR MASTERY
EXPERT TECHNIQUES FOR VIRTUALIZATION
PROFESSIONALS

ROB BOTWRIGHT

Chapter 1: Introduction to Citrix Hypervisor

Troubleshooting common issues in Parallels Desktop is an essential skill for maintaining a smooth and trouble-free virtualization experience. Even with careful configuration and planning, occasional problems can arise, and knowing how to diagnose and resolve them is crucial. This chapter will explore some of the common issues that Parallels Desktop users may encounter and provide troubleshooting steps to address them. One common issue that users may encounter is slow VM performance. If your virtual machine (VM) is running sluggishly or experiencing delays, several factors could be contributing to the problem. One possible cause is inadequate hardware resources allocated to the VM. To address this, you can adjust the VM's settings to allocate more CPU cores, RAM, or graphics resources if your Mac's hardware allows for it. Additionally, consider closing any unnecessary applications running on your Mac to free up system resources for the VM. Another factor that can impact VM performance is disk fragmentation. Over time, the virtual hard disk of your VM may become fragmented, leading to slower read and write speeds. Parallels Desktop provides a built-in feature to optimize disk space, which can help improve performance. Running the disk optimization tool periodically can prevent fragmentation and maintain VM performance. Furthermore, ensure that your Mac's storage drive has sufficient free space, as low disk space can affect both the host and VM performance. If you are experiencing network-related issues within your VM, such as a lack of internet connectivity or problems accessing local network resources, several troubleshooting steps can help resolve these problems. First, check your VM's network configuration to ensure that it is correctly set up. Make sure the network mode (e.g., Shared, Bridged, Host-Only) is appropriate for your needs and that you have selected the correct network adapter type. Additionally, confirm that any firewalls or security software within the VM are not blocking network traffic. If you are using a bridged network mode and experiencing connectivity issues, verify that your host operating system's network settings are configured correctly. Sometimes, the host firewall or network settings can impact the VM's ability to communicate with the network. Another common issue users encounter is sound-related problems within their VMs. If you are experiencing no sound or poor sound quality, there are several troubleshooting steps to follow. First, ensure that the sound settings within the VM are configured correctly. Check that the correct audio output device is selected, and the volume is adjusted appropriately. If sound issues persist, verify that the Parallels Tools are installed and up-to-date within the VM. Parallels Tools include drivers and utilities to enhance VM performance and functionality, including sound support. Updating Parallels Tools can resolve compatibility issues and improve sound quality. If you are still experiencing sound problems, consider checking the host operating system's sound settings to ensure that they are not affecting the VM's audio. Another common challenge is software compatibility issues. VMs running different operating systems and software applications may encounter compatibility problems. For example, Windows-based software running in a VM on a Mac may not function correctly or experience compatibility issues with macOS. In such cases, check for software updates or patches for the problematic application or consult the software vendor's support resources. Additionally, consider running the software in a compatibility mode or virtual machine configuration that better supports the application. Sometimes, problems arise during the installation or update of the Parallels Desktop software itself. If you encounter errors during installation or experience issues when updating Parallels Desktop to a new version, there are steps you can take to troubleshoot these problems. First, ensure that you have a stable internet connection during the installation or update process, as interruptions can lead to incomplete installations. If you encounter errors or installation failures, consult the Parallels Desktop documentation or support resources for specific error code explanations and solutions. Sometimes, resolving these issues may require manually removing existing Parallels Desktop components before reinstalling the software. Additionally, ensure that your macOS is up-to-date and that your Mac meets the system requirements for the Parallels Desktop version you are using. For users who rely on virtual machines for critical work or sensitive data, data loss or corruption is a significant concern. If you encounter data-related problems within your VM, such as missing files or corrupted data, it's essential to have a robust backup and recovery strategy in place. Regularly back up your VMs to ensure that you can recover data in case of unexpected issues. In addition to local backups, consider using cloud-based backup solutions for added data protection. Furthermore, implement proper security practices within your VMs to minimize the risk of malware or data breaches that could result in data loss. If you are experiencing crashes or instability within your VM, diagnosing the root cause is essential to resolving the issue. Crashes can occur for various reasons, including incompatible software, driver issues, or resource constraints. To troubleshoot crashes, review any error messages or logs provided by the VM or the host operating system. These messages can often provide valuable information about the cause of the crash. Additionally, consider updating or reinstalling the guest operating system or specific software applications within the VM to address compatibility issues. If crashes persist, check for driver updates or conflicts that may be causing system instability. In cases where a specific application within the VM is crashing, consult the application's support resources for troubleshooting guidance. Parallels Desktop offers snapshots as a valuable tool for mitigating the impact of crashes or unexpected issues. Taking regular snapshots of your VM allows you to revert to a stable state in case of problems. Snapshots capture the VM's entire state, including the operating system, software, and data, allowing you to roll back to a known-good configuration. Using snapshots as part of your troubleshooting strategy can help you quickly recover from issues and minimize downtime. Finally, if you encounter issues that you cannot resolve through troubleshooting, consider reaching out to Parallels Desktop's support or community resources. The Parallels Desktop community and support teams can provide guidance and assistance for resolving complex or persistent problems. Documenting the issue, including any error messages or log files, can help support teams understand the problem and provide more effective assistance. In summary, troubleshooting common issues in Parallels Desktop requires a systematic approach to diagnose and resolve problems that may arise during virtualization. These issues can include slow VM performance, network connectivity problems, sound-related issues, software compatibility challenges, installation or update errors, data-related concerns, crashes, and more. By following troubleshooting steps, checking configurations, updating software, and maintaining backups, users can address most common issues and maintain a stable virtualization environment. In cases where problems persist, reaching out to Parallels Desktop support or community resources can provide additional assistance in resolving complex issues.

Chapter 2: Installing and Configuring Citrix Hypervisor

Understanding the role of Citrix Hypervisor in virtualization is essential for anyone looking to harness the power of virtual environments for their organization. Citrix Hypervisor, formerly known as XenServer, is a robust virtualization platform that plays a vital role in modern data centers and cloud computing environments. At its core, Citrix Hypervisor provides the foundation for creating and managing virtual machines (VMs) that run multiple operating systems on a single physical host. This capability is central to achieving efficient resource utilization, enhanced scalability, and improved infrastructure flexibility. One of the key roles of Citrix Hypervisor is to abstract physical hardware resources, such as CPU, memory, storage, and network interfaces, into virtual resources that VMs can use. By doing this, it enables the efficient sharing and allocation of these resources among multiple VMs. This abstraction layer allows organizations to run various workloads and applications independently within isolated VMs, ensuring that they do not interfere with one another. Citrix Hypervisor provides a secure and stable environment for hosting VMs, making it suitable for diverse use cases, from server consolidation to application testing and development. An important aspect of Citrix Hypervisor's role is its support for various guest operating systems, including Windows, Linux, and others. This versatility allows organizations to run a wide range of applications and services within VMs, regardless of the operating system they require. Citrix Hypervisor ensures compatibility with popular guest operating systems and provides optimized drivers and tools to enhance VM performance. Another vital role of Citrix Hypervisor is its ability to manage VMs efficiently. It offers features like live VM migration, which allows VMs to be moved from one physical host to another without disrupting operations. This capability is particularly valuable for load balancing, resource optimization, and minimizing downtime during maintenance or hardware upgrades. Citrix Hypervisor also provides dynamic memory management, enabling VMs to allocate and release memory as needed, ensuring optimal resource utilization. This flexibility is crucial for environments with varying workloads and resource demands. In addition to efficient VM management, Citrix Hypervisor offers robust networking capabilities. It provides virtual switches and networking features that allow administrators to create, configure, and manage virtual networks within the hypervisor. This feature is essential for isolating traffic, implementing network policies, and ensuring VMs can communicate securely with each other and external networks. Moreover, Citrix Hypervisor supports advanced networking features like VLAN tagging, NIC bonding, and virtual LANs (VLANs), enabling organizations to build complex network topologies within their virtualized environments. Another significant role of Citrix Hypervisor is its contribution to data center consolidation. By virtualizing multiple physical servers into VMs running on a single host or cluster of hosts, organizations can achieve higher server utilization rates, reduce hardware costs, and minimize data center footprint. This consolidation leads to more efficient resource allocation and management, resulting in cost savings and improved infrastructure efficiency. Citrix Hypervisor's role extends beyond traditional server virtualization. It is well-suited for creating virtual desktop infrastructure (VDI) environments. VDI allows organizations to deliver virtual desktops to end-users, providing flexibility and centralized management. Citrix Hypervisor can host VMs running Windows or Linux desktop operating systems, enabling organizations to tailor virtual desktops to their specific needs. VDI deployments can enhance user productivity, simplify desktop management, and provide better security and data protection. Citrix Hypervisor also plays a vital role in disaster recovery and business continuity. It offers features like VM snapshots and replication, allowing organizations to create backup copies of VMs and replicate them to remote locations. In case of hardware failures or data center outages, these replicated VMs can be quickly activated, minimizing downtime and data loss. This role is critical for organizations that require high availability and robust disaster recovery plans. Furthermore, Citrix Hypervisor's role in cloud computing is noteworthy. It is often used as the virtualization platform in cloud service providers' infrastructures to deliver Infrastructure as a Service (IaaS). Citrix Hypervisor's scalability, resource management, and multi-tenancy support make it an excellent choice for building and managing cloud environments. It enables cloud providers to offer virtualized resources to customers, allowing them to deploy and manage their VMs in the cloud. In summary, Citrix Hypervisor's role in virtualization encompasses a wide range of critical functions, from abstracting hardware resources to efficient VM management and networking capabilities. Its support for diverse guest operating systems, VDI deployments, and disaster recovery solutions makes it a versatile and valuable tool in modern IT environments. Whether used in data centers, cloud infrastructures, or for specific use cases, Citrix Hypervisor plays an integral role in achieving efficient, flexible, and reliable virtualization solutions.

Preparing your infrastructure for Citrix Hypervisor installation is a crucial step to ensure a smooth and successful deployment of this powerful virtualization platform. Before you begin the installation process, you need to take several important factors into consideration to create a solid foundation for your virtualized environment. One of the first steps in preparing your infrastructure is to assess your hardware requirements. Citrix Hypervisor has specific hardware requirements that must be met to ensure optimal performance and compatibility. You should check the compatibility list provided by Citrix to ensure that your server hardware is on the supported list. Additionally, consider the hardware resources required for the number and type of virtual machines (VMs) you plan to run, including CPU, memory, storage, and network interfaces. Another critical aspect of preparing your infrastructure is ensuring that your network is properly configured. Citrix Hypervisor relies on networking for communication between VMs, as well as for management and data transfer. You should plan your network layout, including IP address assignments, subnets, and VLANs, to meet your organization's requirements. Consider segregating different types of network traffic, such as management, VM traffic, and storage traffic, to optimize performance and security. Additionally, make sure that your network switches and routers are properly configured to support the required network features and protocols. Storage is a fundamental component of any virtualization environment, and preparing your storage infrastructure is essential for a successful Citrix Hypervisor installation. Evaluate your storage needs in terms of capacity, performance, and redundancy. Determine whether you will use local storage, network-attached storage (NAS), or storage area network (SAN) solutions to host your VMs and virtual disks. Ensure that your storage systems are compatible with Citrix Hypervisor and that you have sufficient storage capacity to accommodate your VMs and data. Implementing a backup and disaster recovery strategy is another vital aspect of preparing your infrastructure. Having regular backups of your VMs and critical data ensures that you can recover from unexpected failures or data loss. Consider deploying backup solutions that are compatible with Citrix Hypervisor and integrate seamlessly with your virtualized environment. Testing your backup and recovery processes is equally important to ensure they work as expected when needed. In addition to hardware and network considerations, you should also plan for the software components required for Citrix Hypervisor. Ensure that you have a supported operating system installed on your server hardware. Citrix Hypervisor is typically installed on a bare-metal server, so the choice of operating system should align with Citrix's compatibility requirements. Additionally, make sure that your server's firmware and drivers are up-to-date to avoid compatibility issues during installation. Security is a critical aspect of infrastructure preparation. Implementing security best practices and policies ensures that your virtualization environment is protected from potential threats. Consider implementing network security measures such as firewalls, intrusion detection systems, and network segmentation to safeguard your infrastructure. Also, establish strong access controls and authentication mechanisms to control who can manage and access your Citrix Hypervisor environment. Regularly apply security updates and patches to both your server operating system and Citrix Hypervisor to address known vulnerabilities. Monitoring and management tools are essential for maintaining and troubleshooting your virtualized environment. Before installing Citrix Hypervisor, plan for the implementation of monitoring and management solutions that align with your organization's needs. These tools can help you monitor VM performance, track resource utilization, and troubleshoot issues efficiently.

Consider integrating Citrix Hypervisor with centralized management platforms for streamlined administration. As part of your infrastructure preparation, establish a clear plan for user access and permissions within Citrix Hypervisor. Determine who will have administrative access to the virtualization platform and define their roles and responsibilities. Implement role-based access control (RBAC) to restrict access to specific features and functions based on user roles. This ensures that only authorized personnel can make changes to the virtualized environment. Lastly, document your infrastructure configuration and plans thoroughly. Maintain detailed records of hardware specifications, network layouts, storage configurations, and security policies. This documentation serves as a valuable reference for future upgrades, expansions, or troubleshooting efforts. Additionally, consider creating disaster recovery plans and runbooks to guide your response in case of unexpected issues. Preparing your infrastructure for Citrix Hypervisor installation is a critical step in building a reliable and efficient virtualization environment. By carefully assessing hardware requirements, configuring your network, optimizing storage, implementing security measures, and planning for software and management tools, you can create a solid foundation for your virtualized infrastructure. This preparation ensures that your Citrix Hypervisor installation will proceed smoothly and that your virtualization environment will be well-equipped to meet your organization's needs.

Chapter 3: Creating and Managing Virtual Machines

Understanding the basics of virtual machine creation in Citrix Hypervisor is fundamental to harnessing the power of virtualization for your organization's needs. Virtual machines (VMs) are the core building blocks of a virtualized environment, and knowing how to create them is a key skill for any virtualization administrator. The process of creating a VM in Citrix Hypervisor involves several steps that encompass defining VM properties, configuring hardware resources, and installing an operating system. Before you start creating VMs, you should have a clear understanding of the requirements of the workloads you intend to run within them. Begin by determining the operating system and software applications that will be installed on the VM. This information will help you make informed decisions about the VM's hardware configuration and resource allocation. To create a new VM in Citrix Hypervisor, you typically start by launching the Citrix Hypervisor management interface, often known as XenCenter. XenCenter provides a user-friendly graphical interface for managing your virtualized infrastructure. Once XenCenter is open, navigate to the appropriate pool or host where you want to create the VM. Next, you initiate the VM creation process by clicking on the "New VM" or "Create VM" option, depending on your XenCenter version. This action will open a wizard that guides you through the various steps of VM creation. In the wizard, you will need to provide a name for the VM to help identify it within your virtualization environment. Selecting an appropriate name that reflects the VM's purpose can make management and organization more straightforward as you scale your virtual infrastructure. After specifying the VM's name, you will need to choose the VM's location, which typically includes selecting the storage repository where the VM's virtual disks will be stored. This step is crucial for efficient resource allocation and storage management, as it determines where the VM's files will reside. Next, you will be prompted to select the operating system that the VM will run. Citrix Hypervisor offers various pre-defined templates for popular operating systems like Windows, Linux, and more. Choose the template that matches your VM's intended operating system, as this ensures that the VM's settings are optimized for the chosen OS. Additionally, you can specify the amount of memory (RAM) that the VM will be allocated. The amount of RAM you assign to a VM depends on the workload it will run. Ensure that the allocated RAM meets the requirements of your operating system and applications while considering the available resources on the host server. Citrix Hypervisor allows you to configure multiple virtual CPUs for a VM. The number of virtual CPUs should align with the workload's CPU requirements and the available physical CPU cores on the host. Consider the scalability of your virtualized environment, as allocating more virtual CPUs may lead to resource contention if not managed properly. Networking is another crucial aspect of VM creation. You must select a network interface card (NIC) or virtual network for the VM to use. This decision determines how the VM connects to the network and whether it can communicate with other VMs and external systems. Additionally, you can configure advanced networking options, such as VLAN tagging and network bonding, to meet specific requirements. Storage configuration is a vital step in VM creation. You will need to create or select virtual disks for the VM. These virtual disks serve as the VM's storage, and their size should be determined based on the storage requirements of your workload. Citrix Hypervisor supports various storage types, including virtual disk images, physical storage devices, and network-attached storage (NAS) repositories. Select the appropriate storage type and specify the size of the virtual disks accordingly. Citrix Hypervisor allows you to leverage storage features like thin provisioning to optimize storage utilization. In addition to configuring hardware resources, you have the option to enable or disable features such as virtualization extensions and secure boot for the VM. These settings may vary depending on your specific use case and the compatibility of your VM's operating system. After you have configured the VM's properties, you can proceed to install the operating system. This typically involves selecting an installation source, such as an ISO image, a physical DVD drive, or a network-based installation server. The installation source provides the necessary files for the OS installation process. You will need to specify the boot order to ensure that the VM boots from the selected installation source. Once the VM is created and the operating system is installed, you can further customize its settings to meet your specific requirements. This may include installing additional software, configuring network settings, setting up user accounts, and applying security policies. Remember that VM creation is not a one-time task; it's an ongoing process that adapts to the changing needs of your organization. You can create multiple VMs on the same host or distribute them across multiple hosts in a pool to achieve scalability and redundancy. Properly managing and maintaining your VMs is essential for ensuring optimal performance and resource utilization in your virtualized environment. In summary, understanding the basics of virtual machine creation in Citrix Hypervisor involves defining VM properties, configuring hardware resources, and installing an operating system. By following the steps outlined in the VM creation wizard, you can create VMs that meet the specific requirements of your workloads while leveraging the flexibility and efficiency of virtualization.

Chapter 4: Advanced Storage and Networking

Optimizing network connectivity and performance is a critical aspect of managing a virtualized environment effectively. In a virtualized environment, virtual machines (VMs) rely heavily on network connectivity to communicate with each other, external systems, and the broader network infrastructure. To ensure that your virtualized environment operates efficiently, it's essential to optimize network connectivity and performance. One of the first steps in optimizing network connectivity is properly designing the network infrastructure to meet your organization's needs. Consider factors like the number of VMs, expected network traffic patterns, and the need for redundancy and high availability. Plan the layout of your virtual networks, including the creation of virtual LANs (VLANs) to segregate network traffic and isolate different types of communication. Proper network design is the foundation of optimal connectivity and performance. Next, focus on network speed and bandwidth. Ensure that the physical network interfaces (NICs) on your hypervisor hosts are of sufficient speed to handle the expected network traffic. Gigabit or 10 Gigabit Ethernet is common in modern data centers, but your choice may vary based on your specific needs. Consider using multiple NICs and implementing NIC bonding (teaming) to aggregate bandwidth and provide fault tolerance. Optimizing network performance also involves minimizing network latency. Latency can impact the responsiveness of applications and services running on VMs. To reduce latency, use high-quality networking hardware and implement quality of service (QoS) policies to prioritize critical network traffic. Implementing QoS ensures that mission-critical applications receive the necessary network resources, even during periods of high traffic. Another important aspect of optimizing network connectivity is securing your virtualized environment. Implement robust network security measures, including firewalls, intrusion detection systems (IDS), and intrusion prevention systems (IPS), to protect your VMs and data from threats. Segment your network traffic and apply security policies to isolate sensitive workloads and restrict unauthorized access. Encryption of network traffic, particularly for sensitive data, adds an additional layer of security. Citrix Hypervisor offers features like encrypted VM migrations and Secure Boot to enhance network security. Efficiently managing network resources is crucial for optimizing performance. Allocate network bandwidth based on the specific needs of your VMs. Use network resource pools to control and allocate bandwidth to VMs, ensuring that critical workloads receive the necessary resources while preventing resource contention. Additionally, consider implementing network monitoring tools to gain insights into network usage patterns and identify potential performance bottlenecks. These tools can help you proactively address network issues before they impact VM performance. When optimizing network connectivity for VMs, consider the use of virtual switches and network management tools. Citrix Hypervisor provides features like Distributed Virtual Switching (DVS) that allow for centralized control and management of virtual switches. DVS simplifies the configuration and management of network interfaces for multiple VMs, reducing administrative overhead. Efficiently managing IP addresses is essential in a virtualized environment. Implement IP address management (IPAM) solutions or DHCP services to automate IP address assignments and reduce the risk of IP conflicts. Citrix Hypervisor supports both static and dynamic IP address assignments for VMs, giving you flexibility in IP address management. In addition to optimizing network connectivity within your virtualized environment, consider the performance of network storage, as it can significantly impact VM performance. Use network-attached storage (NAS) or storage area network (SAN) solutions that provide high-speed, low-latency access to virtual disks. Ensure that your storage network is properly configured with redundancy and failover capabilities to prevent data loss in case of network failures. Citrix Hypervisor supports various storage protocols, including iSCSI and NFS, allowing you to choose the storage solution that best meets your performance and scalability requirements. Furthermore, optimizing network performance also involves implementing load balancing and failover solutions. Load balancing distributes network traffic across multiple NICs or network paths to ensure even resource utilization and avoid network congestion. Citrix Hypervisor supports network load balancing to improve network performance. Failover solutions, such as NIC teaming and network link aggregation (LAG), provide redundancy and ensure uninterrupted network connectivity in the event of hardware failures. Regularly monitor the health and performance of your network infrastructure to detect and address any issues promptly. Implement network monitoring tools that can provide real-time insights into network performance and help you identify potential bottlenecks. Citrix Hypervisor provides integration with third-party monitoring solutions to facilitate network performance analysis. Finally, stay informed about the latest advancements in networking technologies and best practices for virtualized environments. Networking is a dynamic field, and keeping up with emerging technologies and trends can help you optimize network connectivity and performance in your virtualized environment. In summary, optimizing network connectivity and performance in a virtualized environment is essential for ensuring the efficient operation of virtual machines. This involves proper network design, consideration of network speed and bandwidth, reducing network latency, securing the network, efficient resource management, and monitoring network performance. By implementing these strategies and staying informed about networking trends, you can create a high-performing and reliable virtualized infrastructure.

Chapter 5: High Availability and Load Balancing

Implementing high availability (HA) in Citrix Hypervisor is a critical component of building a resilient and reliable virtualized environment. High availability ensures that your virtual machines (VMs) and applications remain accessible and operational in the event of hardware failures or other disruptions. Citrix Hypervisor provides features and capabilities that enable you to design and implement a high availability strategy tailored to your organization's needs. One of the fundamental concepts in high availability is redundancy. To achieve high availability, you need to eliminate single points of failure by introducing redundancy in your infrastructure. This redundancy can be at various levels, including hardware, network, storage, and even VMs. One common approach to hardware redundancy is using multiple physical servers, often organized in a cluster or pool, to host VMs. Citrix Hypervisor supports server pools, which allow you to group multiple hypervisor hosts together. By distributing VMs across these hosts, you create redundancy in case one host fails. If a host experiences hardware issues or becomes unavailable, the VMs can be automatically migrated to another healthy host within the pool, minimizing downtime. To implement high availability, you should configure and manage VM protection policies. Citrix Hypervisor offers features like HA and VM restart policies that define how VMs should behave when a failure occurs. HA policies determine the actions to take in the event of a host failure, such as VM migration or restart. VM restart policies, on the other hand, specify the order in which VMs should be restarted on available hosts. By defining these policies, you can ensure that critical VMs are prioritized for recovery. Another aspect of high availability is network redundancy. Network failures can disrupt VM communication, so it's essential to plan for network resilience. Implement multiple network paths and configure network bonding or link aggregation to ensure that VMs can continue to communicate even if a network link fails. This redundancy minimizes the risk of network-related disruptions affecting your VMs. Storage redundancy is equally crucial for high availability. Citrix Hypervisor supports various storage solutions, including network-attached storage (NAS) and storage area network (SAN). To achieve storage redundancy, consider implementing features like multipathing and storage failover. Multipathing allows VMs to access storage through multiple paths, ensuring that they can continue to read and write data even if one path fails. Storage failover mechanisms automatically switch to an alternative storage path or device when a failure occurs, further enhancing storage availability. In a high availability configuration, it's essential to regularly monitor the health and performance of your virtualized infrastructure. Implementing monitoring tools that provide real-time insights into the status of your VMs, hosts, and storage can help you detect issues early and take corrective actions. Citrix Hypervisor integrates with monitoring solutions that provide visibility into the performance and availability of your virtualized environment. Testing your high availability setup is crucial to ensure that it functions as expected during actual failures. Conducting regular failover tests allows you to verify that VMs can successfully migrate or restart on alternative hosts, and that network and storage redundancy mechanisms work as intended. By simulating failure scenarios, you can identify and address any potential issues before they impact production environments. Disaster recovery planning is an integral part of high availability. In addition to hardware and software redundancy, you should have a solid disaster recovery plan in place. This plan should include procedures for data backup, off-site storage, and recovery in case of catastrophic events. Citrix Hypervisor supports VM backup and replication solutions that can help you implement disaster recovery strategies. It's important to regularly back up VMs and test the restoration process to ensure that you can quickly recover in the event of data loss or system failures. Another critical consideration for high availability is load balancing. Load balancing distributes workloads evenly across available hosts to optimize resource utilization and prevent resource contention. Citrix Hypervisor provides load balancing features that allow you to evenly distribute VMs across hosts within a pool, ensuring that no single host becomes overloaded. Implementing load balancing contributes to both performance optimization and high availability. In a high availability setup, it's also important to consider licensing and support agreements. Ensure that you have the necessary licenses and support contracts in place to cover the hardware and software components of your virtualized environment. Having access to technical support and updates is crucial for promptly addressing issues and maintaining a reliable high availability configuration. Documentation is a key aspect of implementing high availability. Document your high availability strategy, including details of your HA and VM restart policies, network and storage configurations, monitoring procedures, and disaster recovery plans. Thorough documentation ensures that your team can follow established processes and procedures in the event of a failure. Regularly review and update your documentation to reflect changes in your virtualized environment. Lastly, consider the importance of staff training and expertise in high availability best practices. Ensure that your IT team is well-trained and proficient in managing high availability configurations. Invest in training programs and certifications to keep your staff up-to-date with the latest advancements in virtualization and high availability technologies. In summary, implementing high availability in Citrix Hypervisor is essential for ensuring the reliability and resilience of your virtualized environment. By focusing on redundancy, VM protection policies, network and storage redundancy, monitoring, testing, disaster recovery planning, load balancing, licensing, documentation, and staff expertise, you can create a robust high availability strategy that minimizes downtime and ensures business continuity.

Load balancing techniques are crucial for optimizing the performance and reliability of modern IT infrastructures. In today's highly dynamic and demanding environments, ensuring that workloads are distributed efficiently across resources is paramount. Load balancing helps achieve this by evenly distributing network traffic, computational tasks, or application requests across multiple servers or resources. One of the primary benefits of load balancing is the ability to enhance the availability and fault tolerance of systems. By spreading workloads across multiple resources, load balancers reduce the risk of overloading a single server, thereby reducing the likelihood of system failures and downtime. In essence, load balancing acts as a safety net that catches and redistributes traffic when one server becomes overwhelmed or experiences issues. The most common form of load balancing is known as server load balancing (SLB). SLB involves distributing incoming network traffic across a group of servers to ensure that no single server is overwhelmed, providing high availability and preventing bottlenecks. There are several load balancing algorithms that determine how traffic is distributed. One of the simplest algorithms is round-robin, where each server in the pool takes turns handling requests in a cyclical fashion. While straightforward, round-robin doesn't take into account server load or capacity, which can lead to uneven distribution if some servers are more powerful than others. To address this, weighted round-robin assigns each server a weight based on its capacity, ensuring that more powerful servers handle a proportionally higher number of requests. Another common algorithm is Least Connections, which directs new connections to the server with the fewest active connections, helping to evenly distribute the workload. However, this method doesn't consider server capacity or the complexity of individual requests. To account for server capacity, the Least Response Time algorithm selects the server with the shortest response time, which may indicate lower load. While these algorithms are effective, modern load balancers offer more advanced techniques. One such technique is session persistence or sticky sessions, where the load balancer directs a client's requests to the same server for the duration of their session. This is particularly useful for applications that store session data on the server or for scenarios where maintaining session state is essential. URL-based routing is another technique that enables load balancers to route traffic based on URL patterns. For example, requests to "/images" can be directed to one set of servers, while requests to "/api" can be sent to another group. This allows for more granular control over traffic distribution. Furthermore, content-based routing takes this concept further by examining the content of requests and making routing decisions based on specific content attributes. Content-based routing is valuable when applications need to process and route data differently based on the content type or data payload. Load balancers can also implement health checks to monitor the status of servers. If a server becomes unresponsive or experiences issues, the load balancer can automatically redirect traffic away from that server, ensuring that clients are always directed to healthy resources. In addition to traditional load balancing, modern load balancers can also perform application-aware load balancing. This technique goes beyond basic traffic distribution and understands the structure and behavior of the applications they are serving. Application-aware load balancers can make routing decisions based on application-specific attributes, such as the content of HTTP headers or the payload of application-layer protocols. This level of intelligence allows for more effective load balancing in complex application environments. Global server load balancing (GSLB) is another advanced load balancing technique that distributes traffic across data centers or geographical regions. GSLB takes into account factors like proximity, server health, and data center capacity to ensure that clients are directed to the closest and healthiest resources. This technique is especially valuable for organizations with geographically dispersed users or data centers. Additionally, GSLB can be used for disaster recovery and business continuity planning by automatically redirecting traffic to secondary data centers if the primary one becomes unavailable. In summary, load balancing techniques play a pivotal role in optimizing the performance, availability, and reliability of modern IT infrastructures. These techniques, ranging from basic algorithms like round-robin and weighted round-robin to advanced methods like session persistence, content-based routing, and application-aware load balancing, provide organizations with the tools needed to efficiently distribute workloads across multiple resources. Whether it's enhancing fault tolerance, improving response times, or optimizing resource utilization, load balancing is a critical component of modern computing environments, ensuring that applications and services run smoothly and reliably.

Chapter 6: Snapshots, Cloning, and Templates

Snapshot management is a crucial aspect of maintaining a stable and efficient virtualized environment. Snapshots are point-in-time copies of a virtual machine's (VM) state, including its memory, disk, and settings. They provide a valuable tool for data protection, recovery, and testing in virtualization platforms like VMware, VirtualBox, and Citrix Hypervisor. However, effective snapshot management requires careful planning and adherence to best practices. One of the primary use cases for snapshots is data protection. When you take a snapshot of a VM, you capture its current state, allowing you to revert to that state if something goes wrong. This is particularly useful before making significant changes to a VM or when applying updates or patches. Best practice dictates that you should take a snapshot before making any changes to a VM's configuration or software. Snapshots can also be used for data recovery. If a VM experiences issues or becomes corrupted, you can revert it to a previous snapshot, effectively rolling back to a known-good state. This is especially helpful in troubleshooting scenarios. However, it's essential to remember that snapshots are not a substitute for proper backup solutions. While snapshots can help you recover from certain issues, they are not designed for long-term data retention or disaster recovery. For comprehensive data protection, it's recommended to combine snapshots with regular backups. Another common use case for snapshots is testing and development. You can create a snapshot of a production VM, clone it, and then use the clone for testing purposes. If the testing goes awry or corrupts the VM, you can simply delete the clone and create a new one from the snapshot, ensuring that the production VM remains untouched. Despite their benefits, snapshots also have some limitations and considerations. One of the most critical considerations is snapshot size. Snapshots can consume a significant amount of storage space, especially if a VM undergoes frequent changes. Each snapshot is a delta file that records the changes made since the previous snapshot. Over time, these delta files can accumulate and consume substantial disk space. It's crucial to monitor snapshot sizes and regularly consolidate or delete unnecessary snapshots to reclaim storage. Snapshot consolidation is the process of merging multiple snapshots into a single snapshot or the base VM. Snapshot chains, where each snapshot relies on the previous one, can become complex and lead to performance degradation. Consolidating snapshots reduces the complexity and can improve VM performance. Another consideration is snapshot retention. While snapshots can be helpful for short-term recovery and testing, they should not be kept indefinitely. Over time, managing a large number of snapshots can become cumbersome and impact performance. Establish a snapshot retention policy that defines how long snapshots should be kept and when they should be deleted. Regularly review and enforce this policy to avoid unnecessary storage consumption. Snapshot performance is another aspect to consider. Creating and deleting snapshots can impact VM performance, especially in I/O-intensive environments. When taking a snapshot, the hypervisor briefly suspends the VM to capture its state. During this suspension, VMs may experience downtime or degraded performance. It's essential to plan snapshot operations during maintenance windows or low-activity periods to minimize disruption. Snapshot management best practices also include documenting snapshots. Maintain clear and consistent naming conventions for snapshots, indicating their purpose, date, and relevance. Well-organized snapshot naming helps you quickly identify and manage snapshots. Additionally, consider using annotations or descriptions to provide additional context for each snapshot's purpose. Snapshots should not be relied upon as a long-term backup solution. Regularly back up your VMs using dedicated backup solutions that are designed for data retention and disaster recovery. Snapshots are more suited for short-term recovery, testing, and temporary data protection. It's crucial to understand that snapshots are not a replacement for proper backups. Snapshot management can become complex as your virtual environment grows. To simplify this process, consider using automation and orchestration tools that can help you create, manage, and delete snapshots according to predefined policies and schedules. Automation can streamline snapshot management, reducing the risk of human error and ensuring consistent practices. When using automation tools, ensure that they align with your snapshot retention and naming conventions. In summary, snapshot management is a valuable tool in virtualized environments for data protection, recovery, and testing. However, to make the most of snapshots while avoiding potential pitfalls, it's essential to follow best practices. These include taking snapshots before making changes, using snapshots for short-term recovery and testing, monitoring and managing snapshot size and retention, considering performance implications, documenting snapshots, and understanding their limitations. By adhering to these best practices and combining snapshots with proper backup solutions, you can leverage the full potential of snapshot technology while maintaining a stable and efficient virtualized environment.

Chapter 7: Backup and Disaster Recovery

Developing a comprehensive backup strategy for Citrix Hypervisor is essential for safeguarding your virtualized infrastructure and ensuring business continuity. A robust backup strategy involves careful planning, the selection of appropriate backup methods, and the establishment of clear policies and procedures. The first step in developing a backup strategy is to identify the critical data and virtual machines (VMs) that need to be backed up. This assessment should consider the importance of each VM to your organization's operations and the potential impact of data loss. By prioritizing VMs based on their significance, you can allocate resources and prioritize backup schedules accordingly. Once you've identified the critical VMs, you need to determine the frequency of backups. Some VMs may require daily backups, while others can be backed up less frequently. This decision should be based on factors like data volatility, recovery point objectives (RPOs), and available storage resources. Next, consider the backup methods and technologies that Citrix Hypervisor supports. Citrix Hypervisor offers various backup options, including snapshot-based backups, virtual machine exports, and integration with third-party backup solutions. Snapshot-based backups are a common choice as they provide point-in-time copies of VMs, enabling quick and efficient backups and restores. However, it's important to note that snapshots are not a substitute for traditional backups and should be used in conjunction with other methods. Virtual machine exports involve exporting VMs to external storage in a compatible format, making them portable and easy to restore. Third-party backup solutions offer more advanced features and centralized management, making them suitable for larger and more complex environments. When selecting a backup solution, ensure it integrates seamlessly with Citrix Hypervisor and aligns with your backup strategy's requirements. Consider factors like ease of deployment, scalability, support for multiple hypervisors, and data deduplication capabilities. Another critical aspect of backup strategy development is defining retention policies. Retention policies dictate how long backups should be retained and when they should be purged. These policies should align with your organization's data retention and compliance requirements. Retention periods may vary depending on the VM's role and the data it contains. For example, financial data may require longer retention periods than temporary development VMs. Additionally, consider the storage infrastructure for your backups. Select reliable and redundant storage solutions that can accommodate your backup data volume. Backup storage should be separate from production storage to ensure data isolation and protect against potential disasters that could affect your primary storage. Implement backup storage with redundancy and backup copies stored offsite to enhance data availability and disaster recovery capabilities. Automation plays a crucial role in backup strategy development. Leverage automation tools to schedule and orchestrate backup jobs, reducing the risk of human error and ensuring consistent backups. Automation also simplifies the management of backup policies and retention schedules, making it easier to enforce best practices. Regular testing and validation of your backup strategy are essential. Conduct recovery drills to ensure that backups can be successfully restored and that recovery time objectives (RTOs) are met. Testing also helps identify and address any issues or gaps in your backup strategy. Additionally, establish a clear and well-documented procedure for initiating and monitoring backup jobs. This documentation should include step-by-step instructions for backup and recovery processes, ensuring that your IT team can quickly respond to data loss incidents. Consider the security aspects of your backup strategy. Data encryption, both in transit and at rest, is vital to protect sensitive information during backup and storage. Ensure that your backup solution supports encryption and complies with industry standards for data security. Authentication and access control are equally important. Only authorized personnel should have access to backup data and recovery procedures. Implement strong authentication mechanisms and role-based access controls to safeguard backup infrastructure. Regularly audit and review user access to maintain security. Finally, maintain compliance with relevant regulations and standards. Ensure that your backup strategy aligns with industry-specific compliance requirements, such as GDPR, HIPAA, or PCI DSS, if applicable to your organization. Regularly review and update your backup strategy to adapt to changes in your virtualized environment, business needs, and technological advancements. By continually optimizing and refining your backup strategy, you can maintain the resilience and data protection necessary to support your organization's operations effectively.

Disaster recovery planning and execution are critical components of any organization's overall business continuity strategy. A well-designed disaster recovery plan (DRP) ensures that a business can continue its essential functions even in the face of unexpected and disruptive events. These events can range from natural disasters like hurricanes and earthquakes to technological failures or cyberattacks. The first step in disaster recovery planning is to assess the organization's risk profile. This involves identifying potential threats and vulnerabilities that could impact the business's operations. The assessment should consider both internal and external factors, such as the geographical location of the organization, the industry it operates in, and the types of data it handles. Based on this assessment, the organization can prioritize its disaster recovery efforts and allocate resources accordingly. The next crucial aspect of disaster recovery planning is defining recovery objectives. This includes establishing recovery time objectives (RTOs) and recovery point objectives (RPOs) for different systems and processes. RTO represents the maximum allowable downtime for a system or process, while RPO defines the acceptable data loss in the event of a disaster. These objectives should align with the organization's business needs and regulatory requirements. Once the recovery objectives are set, the organization can develop a comprehensive disaster recovery strategy. This strategy outlines the methods and techniques to be used in the event of a disaster. It should cover various aspects, such as data backup and restoration, system failover and failback, and communication and coordination procedures. A key element of the disaster recovery strategy is the selection of backup and recovery technologies. This may involve implementing data replication, backup solutions, and failover mechanisms that ensure data and systems can be quickly restored in case of a disaster. Testing and validation of the disaster recovery plan are critical to its effectiveness. Regularly conduct disaster recovery drills and simulations to ensure that all personnel understand their roles and responsibilities. Testing helps identify any weaknesses or gaps in the plan and provides an opportunity to refine and improve it. Documentation of the disaster recovery plan is essential to ensure that all stakeholders have access to the necessary information and procedures. This documentation should be kept up to date and readily available to key personnel. In the event of a disaster, clear and well-documented procedures can help minimize downtime and mitigate potential damage. Another critical aspect of disaster recovery planning is the identification of a recovery site. This site serves as a backup location where critical systems and data can be restored and operated if the primary site becomes unavailable. The recovery site can take various forms, from a secondary data center to a cloud-based infrastructure. Selecting the appropriate recovery site depends on factors such as budget, geographic redundancy, and the organization's specific needs. A disaster recovery team should be established and trained to execute the plan effectively. This team should consist of individuals from various departments, each with their own roles and responsibilities during a disaster. Training should include regular exercises to ensure that team members are familiar with the plan and can respond swiftly and efficiently. In addition to technical aspects, communication is a vital component of disaster recovery execution. Establish clear communication channels and contact lists to ensure that all relevant stakeholders can be reached during a disaster. This includes internal teams, external vendors, and third-party service providers. A well-defined communication plan helps coordinate response efforts and keeps everyone informed. Regularly review and update the disaster recovery plan to reflect changes in the organization's infrastructure, technologies, and processes. This ensures that the plan remains relevant and effective over time. It's also important to stay informed about emerging threats and vulnerabilities that could impact the organization's disaster recovery efforts. Cybersecurity threats, in particular, require ongoing vigilance and adaptation of the plan to address new risks. Finally, consider the role of insurance in disaster recovery planning. Business interruption insurance and cyber insurance policies can provide financial protection in the event of a disaster. These policies can help cover the costs of recovery, including data restoration, hardware replacement, and potential legal liabilities. However, it's crucial to review and understand the terms and coverage limits of insurance policies to ensure they align with the organization's recovery objectives. In summary, disaster recovery planning and execution are essential components of a robust business continuity strategy. Organizations must assess their risks, define recovery objectives, develop a comprehensive plan, test and document procedures, establish a recovery team, and maintain open communication channels. Regular updates and adaptability to evolving threats are crucial to ensuring that the disaster recovery plan remains effective. By taking these steps, organizations can enhance their resilience and minimize the impact of disasters on their operations.

Chapter 8: Performance Optimization and Scalability

Performance optimization in Citrix Hypervisor is a critical aspect of managing a virtualized environment efficiently and ensuring the best possible user experience. To achieve optimal performance, organizations should implement a range of strategies and best practices. One of the foundational strategies for performance optimization is proper resource allocation. This involves allocating CPU, memory, storage, and network resources based on the specific needs of each virtual machine (VM). Under-provisioning or over-provisioning resources can lead to performance bottlenecks or inefficient resource utilization. By analyzing the resource requirements of VMs and adjusting allocations accordingly, organizations can ensure that resources are used efficiently. Another essential aspect of performance optimization is monitoring and performance tuning. Continuous monitoring of VM performance metrics allows administrators to identify and address performance issues proactively. Tools like Citrix Hypervisor's built-in monitoring and third-party monitoring solutions can provide insights into resource usage, bottlenecks, and trends. By analyzing this data, administrators can make informed decisions to optimize VM performance. Performance tuning involves adjusting various settings and parameters to fine-tune the virtualized environment. For example, optimizing CPU scheduling and memory ballooning can improve resource utilization. Additionally, administrators can configure storage and network settings to enhance throughput and reduce latency. Another critical strategy is workload balancing. Workload balancing involves distributing VMs across host servers to evenly distribute resource usage. Citrix Hypervisor offers features like XenServer's workload balancing (WLB), which automatically migrates VMs to balance resource usage. Load balancing can prevent resource contention and ensure that no single host server is overloaded. Storage optimization is also a key consideration for performance. Implementing storage technologies like thin provisioning and deduplication can help reduce storage overhead and improve overall efficiency. Using high-performance storage solutions, such as solid-state drives (SSDs), can significantly enhance storage I/O performance. Furthermore, organizations should consider implementing storage management practices like tiering and caching. Network optimization is vital for ensuring optimal performance in a virtualized environment. Utilize features like network bonding and load balancing to increase network bandwidth and redundancy. Implement Quality of Service (QoS) policies to prioritize network traffic and allocate bandwidth appropriately. Additionally, network segmentation and VLANs can isolate traffic and improve network performance and security. Regularly updating and patching Citrix Hypervisor and its components is crucial for performance optimization. Updates often include bug fixes, performance improvements, and security enhancements. Staying current with Citrix Hypervisor updates helps maintain a stable and efficient virtualized environment. Another strategy for performance optimization is leveraging virtualization-aware applications. Citrix Hypervisor supports virtualized applications that are designed to run efficiently in virtualized environments. By using these applications, organizations can benefit from improved performance and resource utilization. Optimizing guest operating systems is equally important. Ensure that guest VMs are running the latest updates and patches to address security vulnerabilities and performance issues. Disable unnecessary services and background processes to reduce resource consumption. Furthermore, consider using Citrix Hypervisor tools for guest VM optimization, such as XenTools for Windows VMs. Effective management of snapshots is essential for performance optimization. While snapshots are valuable for data protection, an excessive number of snapshots can impact performance. Regularly review and clean up unused snapshots to minimize storage overhead. Performance testing and benchmarking are essential for identifying bottlenecks and areas for improvement. Conducting performance tests allows organizations to understand the limits of their virtualized environment and make informed decisions about resource allocation and optimization. Consider using synthetic workloads and benchmarking tools to assess performance. Automation can streamline performance optimization processes. Implement automation scripts and orchestration tools to automate routine tasks like resource allocation, workload balancing, and performance tuning. Automation ensures consistency and reduces the risk of human error. Finally, organizations should establish performance baselines and KPIs (Key Performance Indicators) to monitor and measure the success of their performance optimization efforts. These baselines provide a reference point for evaluating the impact of changes and improvements. By setting specific performance goals and regularly assessing performance against those goals, organizations can maintain a high-performing virtualized environment. In summary, performance optimization in Citrix Hypervisor is a multifaceted process that involves resource allocation, monitoring, tuning, workload balancing, storage and network optimization, software updates, virtualization-aware applications, guest VM optimization, snapshot management, performance testing, automation, and performance benchmarking. By implementing these strategies and best practices, organizations can ensure that their virtualized environments run efficiently, delivering the best possible performance to users while maximizing resource utilization and minimizing potential bottlenecks and downtime. Scaling your Citrix Hypervisor environment is a crucial aspect of managing a growing virtual infrastructure and ensuring it meets the evolving needs of your organization. As your business expands, you may need to add more virtual machines (VMs), host servers, and other resources to accommodate increased workloads and user demands. Scaling effectively requires careful planning and consideration of various factors. One fundamental consideration is the assessment of your current infrastructure and its capacity. Before scaling, evaluate your existing host servers, storage, network, and resource utilization. Identify any performance bottlenecks, resource constraints, or areas that may require enhancement. This assessment provides a baseline understanding of your current environment and helps inform your scaling strategy. When planning to scale your Citrix

Hypervisor environment, consider the anticipated growth of your organization. Forecast your future resource requirements by analyzing historical data and growth trends. This projection will guide your decisions regarding the number of host servers, storage capacity, and networking capabilities needed to accommodate future workloads. Scalability is a key aspect of Citrix Hypervisor, as it allows you to add more host servers and VMs as your needs evolve. To scale out, you can simply add additional host servers to your virtualization cluster. Citrix Hypervisor supports various clustering and pooling options, allowing you to seamlessly integrate new servers into your existing environment. When adding host servers, consider factors such as hardware compatibility, performance, and redundancy. To optimize resource allocation and scalability, make use of Citrix Hypervisor's resource pooling features. Resource pools enable you to group host servers with similar capabilities and allocate resources dynamically within the pool. This approach enhances resource utilization and simplifies management as you scale. Consider implementing high availability (HA) and load balancing as part of your scaling strategy. HA ensures that VMs remain available even in the event of a host server failure. Load balancing distributes VMs across host servers to prevent resource contention and optimize performance. Implementing HA and load balancing mechanisms enhances the resilience and reliability of your virtual infrastructure. Storage scalability is a critical consideration when expanding your Citrix Hypervisor environment. As you add more VMs and data, ensure that your storage infrastructure can accommodate the increased capacity and I/O demands. Consider using storage technologies like network-attached storage (NAS), storage area networks (SANs), or hyper-converged infrastructure (HCI) to scale your storage capabilities. Citrix Hypervisor supports features like storage live migration and storage motion, allowing you to move VMs between storage repositories without downtime. Networking scalability is equally important, especially as your virtualized environment grows. Evaluate your network architecture and ensure that it can handle the additional traffic and connectivity requirements. Consider implementing features like network bonding, VLANs, and Quality of Service (QoS) to optimize network performance and segmentation. When scaling, it's essential to maintain a clear and well-documented configuration management process. Document the changes made during the scaling process to ensure consistency and facilitate troubleshooting. Use configuration management tools and version control systems to track and manage configuration changes across your environment. Regularly monitor and assess the performance and health of your scaled Citrix Hypervisor environment. Implement comprehensive monitoring solutions that provide real-time insights into resource utilization, performance metrics, and potential issues. Proactive monitoring allows you to detect and address performance bottlenecks or resource shortages promptly. When scaling, it's also crucial to consider backup and disaster recovery strategies. As your environment grows, the importance of data protection and business continuity increases. Review and update your backup and disaster recovery plans to accommodate the expanded infrastructure and data volumes. Ensure that your backup and recovery solutions are scalable and capable of handling the increased workload. Automation plays a significant role in managing a scaled Citrix Hypervisor environment efficiently. Leverage automation tools and scripts to streamline routine tasks, resource allocation, and provisioning. Automation helps maintain consistency, reduces the risk of human error, and optimizes resource utilization as you scale. Security should always be a top priority, even as you expand your virtualized environment. Implement security best practices, including access controls, patch management, and regular security assessments. Scaling may introduce new security challenges, so stay vigilant and adapt your security measures accordingly. Consider integrating threat detection and response solutions to enhance your security posture. Finally, maintain flexibility in your scaling strategy to adapt to evolving technologies and business requirements. Continually review and reassess your infrastructure to identify opportunities for optimization and cost-efficiency. Stay informed about industry trends, emerging technologies, and Citrix Hypervisor updates to make informed decisions about scaling your environment. In summary, scaling your Citrix Hypervisor environment is a dynamic and ongoing process that requires careful planning, resource allocation, scalability considerations, monitoring, security measures, and automation. By following these best practices and remaining adaptable to changing circumstances, you can effectively manage the growth of your virtual infrastructure and ensure it continues to meet the demands of your organization.

Chapter 9: Advanced Security and Access Control

Implementing robust security measures in Citrix Hypervisor is paramount to safeguarding your virtualized environment and protecting sensitive data from potential threats. Virtualization security extends beyond traditional IT security practices and requires a comprehensive approach tailored to the unique characteristics of virtualized infrastructures. One of the foundational elements of virtualization security is ensuring the security of the hypervisor itself. Citrix Hypervisor, like any software, may have vulnerabilities that could be exploited by attackers. To mitigate this risk, it's essential to regularly apply security patches and updates provided by Citrix. Implement a patch management process to keep your hypervisor up-to-date and protected against known vulnerabilities. Additionally, consider leveraging Citrix Hypervisor's role-based access control (RBAC) to restrict access to the hypervisor management interface. RBAC allows you to define granular permissions for administrators and limit access to critical functions. Authentication and authorization are fundamental components of virtualization security. Implement strong authentication mechanisms for accessing the hypervisor and its management interfaces. Consider using multifactor authentication (MFA) to add an extra layer of security, especially for privileged accounts. Furthermore, audit and monitor user activity to detect unauthorized access or suspicious behavior. Another critical aspect of virtualization security is the secure configuration of virtual machines (VMs). Adhere to security best practices when creating VMs, and regularly review and update their configurations. Remove unnecessary services and applications from VMs to reduce the attack surface. Implement security policies and standards for VMs to ensure consistency and compliance. Use templates and automation to deploy VMs with predefined security settings. Securing the network is essential in a virtualized environment. Implement network segmentation to isolate VMs and limit lateral movement for attackers. Consider using virtual LANs (VLANs) and firewalls to enforce network boundaries and control traffic. Implement intrusion detection and prevention systems (IDPS) to monitor network traffic for malicious activity. Encryption is a powerful security measure for protecting data in transit and at rest. Use encryption protocols like SSL/TLS for communication between management interfaces and encrypt sensitive data stored in VMs and on storage devices. Citrix Hypervisor provides features like virtual private networks (VPNs) and encrypted storage repositories to enhance security.

Regularly audit and assess the security of your virtualized environment. Conduct vulnerability assessments and penetration testing to identify and address weaknesses. Perform security audits and compliance checks to ensure that your environment adheres to industry standards and regulations. Implement security information and event management (SIEM) solutions to centralize and correlate security logs and events. SIEM solutions can help detect and respond to security incidents promptly. Data protection is a crucial aspect of virtualization security. Implement data backup and recovery strategies to ensure business continuity in the event of data loss or system failures. Regularly back up VMs and critical data and test the restoration process to verify its effectiveness. Consider implementing data loss prevention (DLP) solutions to monitor and prevent unauthorized data transfers within the virtualized environment. Antivirus and antimalware solutions are essential for protecting VMs from malware threats. Install and maintain security software on VMs to scan for and remove malicious software. Keep antivirus definitions up-to-date to ensure protection against the latest threats. Implement host-based intrusion detection systems (HIDS) to monitor host servers for signs of compromise or unauthorized access. HIDS solutions can detect suspicious activity and generate alerts. Security updates and patches are not limited to the hypervisor but also apply to guest operating systems. Regularly update guest VMs with the latest security patches and software updates. Automate the patching process where possible to ensure timely and consistent updates. Implement security policies and group policies to enforce security configurations on guest VMs. Application control and whitelisting can help prevent the execution of unauthorized or malicious software within VMs. Monitor and log guest VM activities to detect and respond to security incidents effectively. Implement a comprehensive logging and monitoring strategy that includes event logs, performance metrics, and security logs. Use log analysis tools and SIEM solutions to centralize and analyze logs for potential security threats. Regularly review and analyze log data to identify anomalies or suspicious behavior. Implement incident response plans and procedures to address security incidents promptly. Establish a dedicated incident response team and define roles and responsibilities. Document incident response procedures, including communication plans and escalation paths. Conduct tabletop exercises and simulations to ensure that the incident response team is prepared for various scenarios. Security awareness and training are critical for maintaining a strong security posture. Educate administrators and users about security best practices and potential threats. Provide training on how to recognize and report security incidents. Regularly test the effectiveness of security controls through vulnerability scanning and penetration testing. Engage external security experts to perform independent assessments of your virtualized environment's security. Document security policies, procedures, and configurations to maintain a clear and up-to-date record of your security measures. Regularly review and update security documentation to reflect changes and improvements. Finally, stay informed about emerging threats and security trends in virtualization. Subscribe to security advisories, participate in industry forums, and network with peers to share knowledge and best practices. Continuously evaluate and enhance your virtualization security strategy to adapt to evolving threats and technologies. In summary, implementing robust security measures in Citrix Hypervisor is a multifaceted process that involves securing the hypervisor itself, enforcing access controls, securing VM configurations, protecting the network, implementing encryption, auditing and monitoring, data protection, antivirus and antimalware, guest OS security, logging and monitoring, incident response, security awareness and training, testing and assessment, documentation, and staying informed about emerging threats. By addressing each of these aspects comprehensively, organizations can create a secure virtualization environment that safeguards their data, applications, and infrastructure from potential threats and vulnerabilities.

Access control and permissions management are essential components of any virtualization environment, including Citrix Hypervisor, as they dictate who can access resources and perform specific actions within the infrastructure. Access control encompasses the process of identifying users and systems, determining what they are allowed to do, and enforcing those restrictions to maintain security and compliance. In Citrix Hypervisor, access control begins with the management of user accounts and their associated permissions. Administrators must create user accounts for individuals who require access to the hypervisor management interface. These user accounts should be tied to specific roles or groups, each of which has defined permissions. Roles and groups serve as the foundation for granting and managing permissions effectively. Roles are sets of permissions that determine what actions users can perform within the hypervisor environment. Common roles in Citrix Hypervisor include "Read-Only," "VM User," "VM Power User," and "Administrator." Each role grants different levels of access and control over the virtualized infrastructure. Groups are collections of user accounts with similar roles or permissions requirements. By assigning users to groups, administrators can easily manage permissions for multiple users simultaneously. For example, a group named "Storage Admins" might include all users responsible for managing storage-related tasks, and they would share a common set of permissions. Permissions in Citrix Hypervisor are associated with specific objects, such as VMs, host servers, storage repositories, or networks. To control access to these objects, administrators grant or restrict permissions based on roles or directly to individual user accounts or groups. Permissions are granular, allowing fine-tuned control over what actions users can perform on each object. Common permissions include the ability to start, stop, pause, or delete VMs; create or modify networks; and manage storage resources. Implementing the principle of least privilege is a fundamental security practice in access control. This principle dictates that users should only be granted the minimum permissions necessary to perform their job functions and nothing more. By following this principle, organizations reduce the risk of unauthorized or unintended actions that could compromise the security or stability of the virtualized environment. In Citrix Hypervisor, administrators should carefully consider the permissions they assign to each user or group to adhere to the principle of least privilege.

Regularly reviewing and auditing permissions is also crucial. As the virtualized environment evolves, user roles may change, and permissions should be adjusted accordingly. Periodic audits help ensure that permissions remain aligned with users' responsibilities and organizational needs. Citrix Hypervisor provides tools and utilities for administrators to review and manage permissions effectively. Auditing user activities and access attempts is essential for monitoring the security of the virtualization environment. Auditing allows administrators to track who accessed the system, what actions they performed, and when those actions occurred. Audit logs provide a historical record of user activity, which can be invaluable in investigating security incidents or compliance violations. Citrix Hypervisor offers comprehensive auditing capabilities that can be configured to record specific events and activities. Auditing should be enabled and configured to meet the organization's security and compliance requirements. Access control extends beyond user accounts and permissions—it also encompasses managing access to the physical infrastructure that hosts the virtualized environment. Physical security measures, such as access controls, surveillance, and environmental monitoring, are essential to protect the hardware that underpins virtualization. Unauthorized physical access to host servers or storage devices could potentially compromise the security of the virtualized environment. Therefore, organizations should implement strict physical security measures and access controls to safeguard the data center or server room. Regularly reviewing and updating access control policies and permissions is essential for maintaining a secure and efficient virtualization environment. As the organization's needs evolve, so too should the access control strategies. Adjust permissions and roles to accommodate changes in user responsibilities or to align with new security requirements. A proactive approach to access control helps prevent security breaches, unauthorized access, and compliance violations. Automating access control processes can streamline user management and permissions assignment. Citrix Hypervisor provides scripting and automation capabilities that allow administrators to automate repetitive tasks related to user account creation, permissions assignment, and role management. By automating these processes, organizations can reduce the risk of human error and improve the efficiency of access control. In summary, access control and permissions management are critical aspects of maintaining the security and integrity of a virtualization environment like Citrix Hypervisor. Effective access control involves creating user accounts, defining roles and groups, assigning granular permissions, adhering to the principle of least privilege, conducting regular audits, monitoring physical security, and keeping access control policies up-to-date. Automation can further enhance the efficiency and accuracy of access control processes, ensuring that only authorized users can access and manage virtualized resources while protecting against security threats and compliance violations.

Chapter 10: Troubleshooting and Maintenance of Citrix Hypervisor Environment

Identifying and resolving common Citrix Hypervisor issues is essential for maintaining the stability and performance of your virtualization environment. As with any complex software system, Citrix Hypervisor can encounter problems that impact its functionality, and administrators must be equipped to troubleshoot and address these issues promptly. One of the most common issues that administrators may encounter is VM performance degradation. VMs may experience slow response times, high CPU usage, or excessive memory consumption, which can affect the user experience. To resolve performance issues, administrators should first identify the underlying cause. This may involve monitoring resource utilization using Citrix Hypervisor's built-in tools or third-party monitoring solutions. Once the root cause is identified, administrators can take appropriate actions, such as reallocating resources, optimizing VM configurations, or addressing resource contention. Another common issue is VM unresponsiveness or "hangs," where a VM becomes non-operational and does not respond to commands. This can be caused by various factors, including resource exhaustion, misconfigured VMs, or underlying hardware problems. To resolve VM hangs, administrators may need to forcibly shut down the affected VM, investigate logs for error messages, and address any underlying issues. Sometimes, VMs may fail to start or boot properly, resulting in errors or a stuck boot process. This can occur due to misconfigured virtual hardware, corrupted VM images, or incompatible guest OS configurations. To address boot issues, administrators should review VM settings, validate the integrity of VM images, and ensure that guest OS settings are correct. Citrix Hypervisor provides tools for accessing VM console logs, which can be valuable in diagnosing boot problems. Network connectivity problems are another common challenge in virtualized environments. VMs may lose network connectivity due to misconfigured virtual networks, incorrect VLAN settings, or network driver issues. To resolve network connectivity issues, administrators should verify network configurations, check for network driver updates, and inspect the virtual switches and routers within the hypervisor. If VMs are unable to communicate with each other or external networks, it may be due to firewall rules, network segmentation, or routing problems. Administrators should review and adjust network policies to ensure proper communication between VMs and with external resources. Storage-related issues can also impact VMs, leading to data corruption or loss. Common storage problems include storage device failures, data corruption, or insufficient storage capacity. To resolve storage issues, administrators should regularly monitor storage health, implement redundancy and backups, and address any storage device failures promptly. Data integrity checks and file system repairs may be necessary in cases of corruption. Administrators should also consider optimizing storage performance through techniques such as storage tiering or caching. Citrix Hypervisor provides tools for managing storage and diagnosing storage-related problems. Sometimes, administrators may encounter issues related to Citrix Hypervisor updates and patches. Incompatibilities between Citrix Hypervisor versions or between Citrix Hypervisor and guest OS updates can lead to problems. To mitigate update-related issues, administrators should thoroughly test updates in a non-production environment before applying them to critical systems. Additionally, keeping a backup or snapshot of the virtualization environment before updates can facilitate rollback in case of issues. Security vulnerabilities and breaches are a significant concern in virtualized environments. Common security issues may include unauthorized access, malware infections, or vulnerabilities in virtualization software. To enhance security, administrators should regularly apply security patches and updates, enforce access controls, monitor for suspicious activity, and implement security best practices. Security audits and assessments can help identify vulnerabilities and weaknesses. Backup and recovery issues can be disruptive, especially if data loss occurs. Common problems may include failed backups, corrupted backups, or difficulties in restoring VMs. To ensure effective backup and recovery, administrators should regularly test backup procedures, verify backup integrity, and document recovery processes. Citrix Hypervisor provides backup and snapshot features that can simplify data protection. Resource overcommitment, where administrators allocate more resources than the physical infrastructure can support, can lead to performance problems. To address overcommitment, administrators should carefully manage resource allocations, monitor resource utilization, and adjust VM configurations as needed. Resource allocation and monitoring tools in Citrix Hypervisor can assist in optimizing resource usage. Inadequate capacity planning can result in resource shortages and performance issues. Administrators should regularly assess resource demands and plan for scalability by adding more hardware resources when needed. Storage capacity, memory, and CPU resources should be scaled to accommodate future growth. Effective monitoring and performance tuning can help identify and resolve issues proactively. Administrators should use monitoring tools to track resource utilization, detect anomalies, and predict capacity needs. Performance tuning may involve adjusting VM settings, optimizing storage configurations, or fine-tuning virtual networks. Maintaining a thorough understanding of Citrix Hypervisor's features and capabilities is crucial for effective issue identification and resolution. Administrators should continually update their knowledge through training, documentation, and peer collaboration. In complex environments, issues may require escalation to Citrix support or external experts for resolution. Effective communication and documentation of issues and their resolutions are essential for building a knowledge base and facilitating future troubleshooting. In summary, identifying and resolving common Citrix Hypervisor issues is a critical aspect of maintaining a stable and reliable virtualization environment. These issues can encompass performance problems, VM unresponsiveness, boot failures, network connectivity issues, storage problems, update-related challenges, security concerns, backup and recovery issues, resource overcommitment, and inadequate capacity planning. Administrators must possess the skills and knowledge to diagnose and address these issues promptly, ensuring the continued success of the virtualization infrastructure. Ongoing maintenance and monitoring practices are essential for ensuring the health, performance, and security of your virtualization environment. These practices involve a series of proactive and reactive measures that help detect, prevent, and resolve issues that may arise in your Citrix Hypervisor deployment. Regularly updating and patching the Citrix Hypervisor software is a fundamental aspect of ongoing maintenance. New versions and updates often contain bug fixes, security patches, and performance enhancements that can improve the overall stability and security of your virtualization infrastructure. To maintain a secure and up-to-date environment, administrators should establish a routine for applying these updates. However, it's essential to test updates in a non-production environment before rolling them out to critical systems to avoid potential compatibility issues or disruptions. In addition to software updates, hardware components such as servers, storage devices, and network equipment should be regularly maintained and updated. Firmware updates and hardware diagnostics can help address potential hardware-related issues and ensure optimal performance. Regular backups of virtual machines (VMs) and critical data are crucial for data protection and disaster recovery. Administrators should establish backup schedules and procedures that align with the organization's recovery point objectives (RPOs) and recovery time objectives (RTOs). Regularly testing backups by restoring VMs or data to a separate environment helps ensure that data can be recovered when needed. Monitoring is a continuous process that involves tracking various aspects of your virtualization environment. This includes monitoring resource utilization, VM performance, network traffic, and system logs. Effective monitoring can help identify issues before they become critical and allow administrators to take proactive measures. Many monitoring tools and solutions are available, including those provided by Citrix Hypervisor, as well as third-party options. Implementing proper access controls and security policies is essential to protect your virtualization environment. Administrators should regularly review and update access controls to ensure that only authorized users have access to critical resources. In addition to access controls, organizations should implement security best practices, such as network segmentation, intrusion detection systems (IDS), and regular security audits. Security audits can help identify vulnerabilities and weaknesses that may need to be addressed. Implementing network segmentation can isolate VMs based on their roles and sensitivity levels, limiting the potential impact of security breaches. Intrusion detection systems can help detect and respond to unauthorized access attempts and other security threats. Regular security audits can identify vulnerabilities and weaknesses in the virtualization environment and help administrators take corrective actions. Capacity planning is another critical aspect of ongoing maintenance. Capacity planning involves evaluating resource demands and ensuring that the virtualization environment can scale to accommodate future growth. By regularly assessing resource utilization and predicting capacity needs, administrators can proactively allocate additional resources as required, avoiding resource shortages that could lead to performance issues. Routine performance tuning and optimization can help keep the virtualization environment running smoothly. This may involve adjusting VM configurations, optimizing storage and network settings, and fine-tuning resource allocation. Performance tuning should be based on monitoring data and specific performance goals set by the organization. Regularly reviewing and optimizing VM configurations can help ensure that VMs are running efficiently and effectively. This may involve adjusting CPU, memory, and storage allocations, as well as optimizing network settings for the intended workloads. Additionally, administrators should consider implementing resource management features provided by Citrix Hypervisor, such as dynamic memory control and

CPU throttling, to enhance performance. Capacity planning should consider not only the current resource requirements but also the potential growth and scalability needs of the organization. This can involve adding more physical hardware resources, such as servers, storage, and networking equipment, to accommodate future VMs and workloads. Scaling the virtualization environment should align with the organization's strategic goals and anticipated growth. Documentation is a critical component of ongoing maintenance and monitoring. Administrators should maintain comprehensive documentation that includes configuration details, access control policies, security settings, and procedures for common tasks and issue resolution. Documentation serves as a valuable reference for administrators and can expedite issue resolution by providing clear instructions and guidelines. Regularly reviewing and updating documentation is essential to ensure that it remains accurate and reflects any changes or enhancements to the virtualization environment. Disaster recovery planning is a critical aspect of ongoing maintenance. Organizations should have a well-defined disaster recovery plan that outlines how to respond to various scenarios, such as hardware failures, data corruption, or security breaches. The plan should include procedures for data backup and restoration, as well as a clear chain of command and communication protocols during a disaster. Regularly testing the disaster recovery plan through simulated exercises or tabletop drills can help identify weaknesses and ensure that the organization is prepared to respond effectively in a crisis. Maintaining compliance with regulatory requirements is an ongoing responsibility for many organizations. This may involve implementing specific security controls, logging and auditing practices, and data retention policies to meet regulatory standards. Regular audits and assessments can help organizations ensure that they remain compliant with relevant regulations. Administrators should stay informed about changes in regulatory requirements that may impact their virtualization environment and update their practices accordingly. Effective communication and collaboration among IT teams and stakeholders are vital components of ongoing maintenance and monitoring. Administrators should regularly communicate with other IT teams, such as networking, storage, and security, to ensure that the virtualization environment aligns with broader IT strategies and goals. Collaboration can help identify potential issues and ensure that changes or updates to one part of the IT infrastructure do not negatively impact the virtualization environment. In summary, ongoing maintenance and monitoring practices are essential for the successful operation of a Citrix Hypervisor virtualization environment. These practices encompass a range of activities, including regular software and hardware updates, data backups, monitoring, security measures, capacity planning, performance tuning, documentation, disaster recovery planning, regulatory compliance, and effective communication and collaboration. By diligently following these practices, organizations can maintain a stable, secure, and efficient virtualization environment that meets their current and future needs.

Conclusion

In the world of IT and virtualization, knowledge is power, and with the "Virtualization Power Pack: Novice To Ninja," you've embarked on a transformative journey from novice to virtuoso in the realm of virtualization. This bundle, comprising four comprehensive books, has equipped you with the skills and expertise needed to navigate the complex landscape of virtualization technologies.

In "Virtualization Essentials: A Beginner's Guide to VMware" (Book 1), you laid the foundation of your virtualization knowledge. You began as a novice, exploring the fundamental concepts of virtualization, understanding VMware basics, and creating your first virtual machine. You learned to configure virtual networks, manage virtual storage, and even troubleshoot common issues. This book served as your entry point into the world of virtualization, providing you with a strong foothold to build upon.

"Mastering VirtualBox: Building and Managing Virtual Environments" (Book 2) took you deeper into the virtualization realm. You honed your skills by installing VirtualBox, creating virtual machines, configuring virtual networks, and mastering the art of managing virtual storage. This book expanded your virtualization toolkit, allowing you to handle a wider range of scenarios and challenges.

As you progressed to "Advanced Virtualization with Parallels Desktop: Optimizing for Productivity and Performance" (Book 3), you delved into the world of macOS virtualization. You learned how to seamlessly integrate Parallels Desktop with Mac OS, employ advanced storage management techniques, and optimize performance to enhance productivity. This book empowered you to harness the full potential of virtualization on macOS.

Finally, in "Citrix Hypervisor Mastery: Expert Techniques for Virtualization Professionals" (Book 4), you reached the pinnacle of virtualization expertise. You delved into advanced storage and networking, explored high availability and load balancing, and mastered snapshots, cloning, and backup strategies. This book equipped you with the skills needed to manage large-scale virtualization environments with Citrix Hypervisor, solidifying your position as a virtualization ninja.

As you reflect on your journey from novice to ninja, it's clear that virtualization is not merely a technology; it's a powerful tool that can revolutionize the way businesses operate. The knowledge and skills you've gained from this bundle are invaluable, enabling you to optimize resource utilization, improve flexibility, and enhance data security—all while reducing costs.

Whether you're an IT professional seeking to advance your career, an entrepreneur looking to streamline operations, or simply an enthusiast eager to explore the virtual world, the "Virtualization Power Pack: Novice To Ninja" has equipped you with the expertise to excel in the dynamic field of virtualization.

Your journey doesn't end here. Virtualization continues to evolve, and staying up-to-date with the latest developments and best practices is crucial. Remember that your newfound expertise is a stepping stone to even greater heights in the world of virtualization. So, continue to explore, innovate, and harness the power of virtualization to shape the future of technology. Your journey is just beginning, and the possibilities are limitless.

www.ingramcontent.com/pod-product-compliance
Lightning Source LLC
Chambersburg PA
CBHW071236050326
40690CB00011B/2147